I AM
NOT
A CAT!

I AM NOT A CAT!

From avatars to Zoom calls –
the pitfalls of modern life

Tim Collins

Michael O'Mara Books Limited

First published in Great Britain in 2021 by
Michael O'Mara Books Limited
9 Lion Yard
Tremadoc Road
London SW4 7NQ

A CIP catalogue record for this book is available from the British Library.

Papers used by Michael O'Mara Books Limited are natural,
recyclable products made from wood grown in sustainable
forests. The manufacturing processes conform to the
environmental regulations of the country of origin.

ISBN: 978-1-78929-386-9 in paperback print format
ISBN: 978-1-78929-387-6 in ebook format

1 2 3 4 5 6 7 8 9 10

Cover design by Ana Bjezancevic, using an illustration
by Red-Blue Photo on Shutterstock
Illustrations by Andrew Pinder
Designed and typeset by Claire Cater
Printed and bound by CPI Group (UK) Ltd, Croydon, CR0 4YY

www.mombooks.com

CONTENTS

INTRODUCTION

All your colleagues are staring at you. It's time for your big Zoom presentation. Not just to your boss, but to your boss's boss. Your whole career is riding on this. If it goes well, there could be a promotion in it. And one that comes with an actual pay rise, not just a fancy job title.

You begin. And everyone starts laughing. For a moment you're back in school, cringing behind your hands that time you shat yourself on the pommel horse. But what have you done wrong now? That's when you realize. The cat filter your daughter downloaded has switched itself on, and you don't know how to turn it off.

Your colleagues can no longer see a smartly dressed (on the top half, at least) professional, but a white kitten with huge, forlorn eyes. And the irony is that the despairing kitten is expressing your pain in a way that you never could. There's nothing to do but fumble around with your settings and cry, 'I am *not* a cat!' over and over again until you start to believe that, maybe, you *really are* a cat and everything you know as reality is a fever dream triggered by eating a bar of chocolate barnacled with what turned out to be tasty, succulent mould.

Accidentally transforming into a cat is just one of a million strange perils that await you in our strange online world. This book is here to warn you about these new pitfalls. Take care, or the next meme could be YOU.

WORK

Reading Angry Office Emails

Your cocky, smirking work enemy talks over you in meetings and constantly steals the credit for everything that you do. You could have confronted them about their behaviour, or even discussed it with your boss, but you came up with a better solution. Steal their food from the fridge.

They say revenge is a dish best served cold, but it also feels pretty good microwaved.

It started with the theft of a yogurt. This inspired an email rant from them about disrespecting co-workers. They said they'd take things no further if the thief provided a replacement. Did you heck!

Then you struck again. You took their Wotsits, their Tropicana and even their Dairy Milk.

Teams Fail

In 2020, a Twitter user reported that her boss had turned herself into a potato during a Microsoft Teams meeting and couldn't work out how to turn the setting off. Her tweet became so popular that thousands of Teams users downloaded the Snap Camera app so they too could become a potato.

The angry emails got the staff guessing who the villain was, and you even joined in some of these conversations, while secretly congratulating yourself on your criminal genius. Then, a few days ago, you stepped things up. You started scooping the specially prepared meals out of your enemy's lunch box and heating them up for yourself. First some macaroni cheese, then a delicious chicken curry.

Today you've taken their lasagne and are casually eating it at your desk. OK, it's a little crunchy, perhaps overcooked, but it still tastes good, and it will taste even better when you read the angry email your enemy has just sent round. It's shorter than usual. 'To whoever is stealing my food, hope you're enjoying the big toenail-clipping lasagne.'

And you're gagging. You need to spit it into the bin right now. But then everyone will know you're guilty. The only way you'll get away with this is to eat the whole thing and look like you're really enjoying it. Especially the crunchy topping.

Judging Zoom Backdrops

For once, you've spent hours preparing for a meeting. Not that you've done any actual work. You've simply rearranged your vases and lamps neatly on the fireplace behind you, and finally got around to putting up that Matisse print you bought when you moved in.

The meeting begins and you're confident you'll win the Battle of the Rooms. Your first colleague has empty bookshelves behind them. Either they have more shelves than books, which means they're stupid, or they've had to hide their reading material because it's all biographies of serial killers. A stern colleague joins and, amazingly, is sitting in front of a light box with 'Live Laugh Love' on it. You'd have bet anything it would be 'Die Scowl Hate'.

Your boss has their laptop facing a blank wall, which is probably for the best. If it were pointing the other way and you could see their huge living room and the rolling acres of formal gardens beyond their French windows, there would be a workers' uprising.

They ask what you think, and you realize you've been paying no attention whatsoever. You say it's a good idea, and hope the topic isn't your redundancy.

Two other colleagues have classy minimal backdrops like yours, and you feel threatened. They couldn't have beaten you for the Best Room, could they? You decide not. One has lit the candles on their shelves, which is surely trying too hard. This is a Zoom call, not a Dickens novel. The second has fresh flowers behind them. Either they've spent actual money to win the backdrop war, or they've just had a row with their partner. You choose the latter.

Before you know it, the meeting is over. Just as your boss is about to leave, they ask you to write it up. You agree, then remember that you haven't listened to a word anyone said. You'll just have to hope they'll be happy with a report that's entirely about interior décor.

Viral Shame

In 2015, a personalized number plate went viral. It read 'Is♥ed', which was meant to read 'Is loved'. The problem was that most people read it as 'I sharted'.

Accidentally Insulting your Boss

· ·

Frustrated at work, you spend twenty minutes crafting an email to your colleague about how much you hate your boss. You go into great detail – that he reeks like a randy llama, loves meaningless buzzwords and manages to make more money than everyone else combined, while doing less work than the broken stapler at the back of the stationery cupboard.

Getting it all down makes you feel much better, and you send it to your friend. But then something odd happens. Your computer helpfully suggests a list of people you might want to copy in, and you somehow click on one.

Selfie Disaster

In 2012, a woman's sexy bathroom selfie went viral because she'd accidentally left her diarrhoea medicine next to the mirror.

Your pulse explodes, your stomach erupts. You've just pinged the email to your boss. You've told the one person who stands between you and sleeping in a doorway the truth about himself. There's no way this can end well.

You glance over at your boss's office, and there's a flicker of hope. Your boss is still away for lunch at 2.45p.m., and he has left his laptop open. Surely no one would notice if you popped in and deleted the offending email?

You edge across the floor with beads of sweat trickling down your forehead. You swing open the door. The laptop is right there, in front of you. You press enter, and the screensaver disappears with no password request. You click on your email … scroll up to the trash icon … the floorboards are creaking. The heavy footsteps of your boss are approaching. You watch with terror as he barges in, early, back from lunch.

He scowls at you, demanding an explanation. There must be a million ways you could talk yourself out of this. But not a single one enters your befuddled brain. You go for the only option you can think of, which is to grab his laptop and hurl it out of the window. There's a crunch on the street miles below.

Somehow, you've managed to make things even worse.

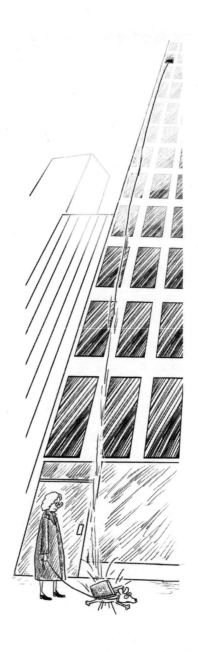

Screen-sharing

It's your turn to present on Zoom. You open PowerPoint and click the 'share screen' option. It's all going well until a message appears on the top of the screen. 'Can I see you tonight?'

Uh-oh. You'd forgotten to turn off the chat notifications. Now the whole office is reading the private message, and it's going to be a lot more entertaining than your presentation.

'That's from my husband,' you lie. You try to move on, but another message appears: 'My wife's out.' 'He's means *me*,' you say. 'That's his way of reminding me about my spin class.' Your colleagues look distracted, but if you can get back to the presentation, you could win them over.

And then: 'Bring the toys.'

'He means the Lego for our son,' you say. 'I'm so glad he reminded me.'

You should really close PowerPoint and change

your notification settings. But you can't, because then your boss would see the 'New Job Applications' folder on your desktop. You're just going to have to style this out.

Then: 'And the lube.'

'That's what he calls his lubricated eye drops,' you say, thinking on your feet. 'He has dry eye.' Everyone is gazing at you in horror. You've never given a presentation that's held their attention like this. Hang on, *not* everyone. Josh is typing on his phone and scowling.

The same Josh who's friends with your actual husband.

Twitter Fail

A man in the US messaged Dominos on Twitter to tell them that his pizza had arrived with 'no topping on it' and was 'just bread'. In his next tweet, he admitted that he'd opened the box upside down.

Having Your Zoom Call Interrupted by Your Child

Delivering an important presentation while looking after your child is going to be tough. It's time to step up the parenting skills.

You try to explain the situation to your child, telling them they need to be quiet for thirty minutes while you do some important work on your computer. They initially agree, but then threaten to run in and shout, 'Farty farty farty fart-fart'. Cue a series of tense negotiations, and you end up pledging three extra hours of screen time, five chocolate cakes and Disneyland in exchange for their cooperation. Done deal.

Watching the clock in the top right corner of your screen as you present, you begin to feel hopeful: ten minutes pass, twenty. Could you actually have pulled this off? But you're interrupted by sniggers five minutes from the end, and you turn around to see your offspring peeping around the door. You ask to be excused for a minute and go over to give them what looks like a stern telling-off, but is actually a desperate attempt to add more toys and chocolate into the bargain. But they're bored, so they'll have to spend the rest of the presentation on your lap.

Text Fail

An office worker in the US texted her boss to ask if she could take time off for a funeral. Due to an autocorrect error, he responded, 'Of corpse'.

Zoom Fail

A Zoom mishap caused a Republican lawmaker to appear at the House of Representatives as a floating upside-down head. A committee meeting had to be paused as he worked out how to get himself the right way up again.

You get through it, and ask if anyone has any questions. Your child does. They ask you which of the people on the screen is the one you call 'Twatface'. Now everyone on Zoom is laughing. Everyone, that is, except Twatface.

Maybe you should work from home permanently now. At least it means you'll never have to explain yourself to Twatface.

Accidentally Revealing Your Secret Crush

You fancy the person who sits opposite, but there's no way you can ever tell them. You're fated to do nothing but glance sneakily at their Facebook profile and wish you could be together. You type their name into the search bar and press enter. You're immediately struck with a sense that something has gone horribly wrong. But what?

You've posted their name as a status update, that's what. You scrabble around and manage to delete it, but too late. Your friends, relatives and vague acquaintances have all just seen directly into your soul.

Over on the other side of the office, Brad from Finance is grinning. He's pointing at you and telling Jade something. Now they're both laughing. Your secret is out. And if your crush is going to hear it anyway, they might as well hear it from you. You stride over to the kitchen area, where they're taking their lunch out of the fridge.

You apologize for accidentally sharing their name as your status. *And* accidentally liking their holiday snaps last night. *And* the night before. But well … look … what you're trying to say is … gosh, this is hard … you *love* them.

You wait for them to toss their lunch aside and embrace you. But they use it as a shield, edging around you to keep as much space as possible. Now your crush sits thirty desks away from you, and they've unfriended you. That's what you get for telling Facebook what's really on your mind.

Instagram Shame

An Instagram user posted a picture of herself looking surprised in the shower with the caption, 'My boyfriend is always sneaking up on me!' However, the reflection in the bathroom mirror revealed that she'd actually taken the shot herself.

Using Autocorrect

· · · · · · · · · · · · · · · · · · ·

You attempt to text a colleague while rushing to a meeting. It would be difficult enough if your fingers weren't sticky from the can of Coke you're sipping. But the message must be sent. You text, 'Need to see you in the meeting room at 2.50 for brief conference.'

Your colleague replies, 'WTF?' You look back at the conversation and see that autocorrect has changed it to, 'Need to see you in the meeting room at 2.50 for brief cunnilingus.' What was that word even doing in your phone's dictionary? You apologize and send the correct message. You add, 'Also, Jasmine needs to be there too, can you find her?'

Your colleague texts, 'Seriously?' You look back and see that your phone changed it to, 'Also, Jasmine needs to be there too, can you finger her?' You reply, 'Having trouble typing. My hand is sticky because of Coke.' Your colleague says, 'I'm ending this conversation'. You look back and see your phone changed it to, 'Having trouble typing. My hand is sticky because of cock.'

Never mind. You'll be back at the office soon, and you'll be able to apologize to her in person, where everything you say isn't translated into unpleasant erotica by your unhelpful phone. But when you arrive at the meeting room, your colleague is nowhere to be seen. The only person there is your boss, waiting to give you a formal warning.

Text Fail

A woman in the US texted the message, 'Daddy's in Heaven' to all her children. She had meant to attach a picture of him with his new boat.

Tweeting a Meeting

As far as you know, your boss hasn't installed CCTV in your house yet. So you can use Twitter during your dull Zoom meeting and it will look exactly like you're taking notes. You start typing:

🐾 I'm pretending to be writing notes on a shitty work meeting.

🐾 This might not be very interesting for you. On the other hand, you might want to know what it looks like the exact moment someone loses their will to live.

🐾 Great. Karen has just asked a question. Now we all have to ask one or look bad.

🐾 Who asks a question when a meeting is already overrunning? That takes five minutes off my lunch break, which means I'm going to have to cancel one of my starters.

🐾 My firm's plan is to ensure loyalty by filling us with so much inertia we can't be bothered to look for other jobs. It's working well.

🐾 I was refused a half-day holiday for this. It was just SO important that I should be sitting here, squinting at the camera while actually planning how to rearrange my lounge.

🐾 If I made a loop of myself nodding and occasionally saying 'yes', would I get away with it?

🐾 And it's over. Now for fifty-five minutes of solid eating before the whole shitshow starts again.

You close Zoom and are about to exit Twitter when you notice you have eight notifications. Maybe you're going viral. Maybe you can quit your job and become a full-time social media rockstar.

You click on them. Your tweets were all liked by the same person. Your boss. Oh yeah. You forgot they were following you.

Getting Work Emails at Odd Times

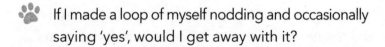

A new member of your team has joined and they're pretending to be a workaholic. They email you at bizarre times, and you know they're just doing it to make themselves look dedicated. You can forgive a late evening email from someone in an overseas office. But *this snake* sits directly across from you.

You're just settling down with a glass of wine and the Netflix menu when you get a notification. Snake wants to know if you'd like to check a meeting report. You wouldn't, obviously, but the nagging sense that you're meant to be doing it ruins your evening.

A weekend walk in the park, and thoughts about work are finally floating away. You absent-mindedly check your emails, and Snake has got in touch to tell you about a business bestseller they've been reading. You see Snake's smug face in every cloud and tree for the rest of the day.

Facebook Fail

A couple who announced their engagement on Facebook in 2015 might have given away more than they intended. Although the woman was pointing at her new ring, most of the comments were about the pregnancy test that could be seen in the lower right-hand corner.

One morning you wake up to a request to look over Snake's PowerPoint slides before the 9a.m. meeting. What exactly do they want you to sacrifice from your morning routine? Brushing your teeth? Having a piss?

Sick of it all, you decide to call their bluff. You set an alarm for 5a.m., and call Snake to ask what they think the company's strategy should be for the next quarter. You realize something is wrong when you hear a tapping keyboard and get a cheery greeting from Snake.

Oh god. They really are a workaholic. You thought they were just putting it on and you were wrong. Now you're actually having a meeting at a time when only badgers and burglars are awake. And don't think it will be the last one – now they've got you down as someone else who enjoys a cheeky all-nighter.

Text Fail

A Twitter user shared an alarming text from her mother that read, 'Your great aunt just passed away. LOL.' Apparently, she thought it stood for 'Lots of Love'.

Sending a Job Application

· · · · · · · · · · · · · · · · · ·

You've worked on your CV all day, and it's perfect. After all, what sort of company could resist someone who's fluent in both Word and PowerPoint, has French GCSE and enjoys going to restaurants? You even copied and pasted an inspirational quote at the end of your personal statement. If this company doesn't want you, they deserve to go under.

You check your cover email and hit send. Now you just have to sit back and prepare for the salary negotiations.

A quick glance at your 'sent messages' folder reveals a slight problem. You didn't actually attach your CV. Not a great move from someone who just boasted about their attention to detail. You send another email, explaining that it's the first time you've ever done anything like that, and you promise it won't happen when you work for them. BUT you realize you still haven't actually sent them your CV, so you try a third time. Unfortunately, you accidentally attach a photo of a water-skiing squirrel instead.

Tenacity is important in business, and you're sure your future employers will understand that as they wade through your messages. So you try again, and *finally* manage to attach your CV.

You're about to shut your laptop down when you notice another small error. You've emailed it to your current boss.

Twitter Cringe

In 2017, a Twitter user admitted that he broke up with his girlfriend in a restaurant, and she started crying. All the other customers thought he'd proposed, and they applauded.

Writing a Passive-Aggressive Email

· · · · · · · · · · · · · · · · · ·

Your lazy colleague is slouching back in their chair on the other side of the office. They start to move. Are they about to do that simple task you gave them one week ago? No, they're pulling a Nerf gun out from under their desk so they can fire a soft orange pellet at the receptionist.

You tense up, and realize you're going to have to get your rage out somehow. It's time for a passive-aggressive email. You consider a devastating title like 'Quick Reminder', but that wouldn't be enough punishment so you find your original email in your sent folder and fire it to them.

You begin, 'Not sure if you got a chance to look at this', even though you know they've had plenty of chances. They could have done it instead of organizing that wheelie chair grand prix last Wednesday, for a start. And continue, 'I'm just wondering how you're getting on with the report?' You aren't wondering. You know they've done nothing.

Zoom Fail

In perhaps the most famous Zoom fail of all, Texan lawyer Rod Ponton got stuck behind a cat filter during an online court hearing. Millions have watched the footage of him appearing as a sad white kitten and saying, 'I am not a cat. I'm live here.'

Your teeth grind and the veins in your forehead throb as you hit them with veiled barbs like 'Let me know if you need anything else', 'Perhaps it was my fault for not being clear enough', and 'I hope you don't mind that I'm CC-ing Charlotte on this'. Sweat drips down your temples as you finish with the brutal 'Thanks in advance'. It's harsh, but it still isn't enough to fully articulate your rage.

Over on the other side of the office, your colleague has now started a conversation about international variations of chocolate bars, which will no doubt distract everyone until lunch. Unable to stop yourself, you add, 'LOOK JUST DO SOME WORK FOR ONCE IN YOUR LIFE, YOU LAZY BASTARD', and press send.

This is bad. You've failed to mask your wrath and have become the workplace bully. At least you sent it to someone who could never be bothered to take you to a tribunal.

Drunk Emailing

Your appraisal didn't quite go the way you hoped. Your boss agreed that you're doing well in your role, but refused to give you a promotion or a pay rise. They wouldn't even give you that bigger monitor you asked for. You can't help but wonder if things would have gone better if you'd been more assertive.

You're feeling much bolder after a night in the pub. If only you could have your appraisal now. Wait a minute. You can. You've got an email app on your phone, haven't you? You open it. Showing you mean business, you begin the email 'Dear twat'. You finally have the chance to say everything you wanted to earlier. 'I am brilliant,' you continue. 'Give me some more money.'

Viral Shame

A Christian bumper sticker featured a cross next to the word 'unashamed'. Unfortunately, the cross looked like a 't', so that the sticker read, 'tunashamed', causing many to wonder how you could possibly shame a tuna.

You know you have to give reasons in an appraisal, so you add, 'You've got a BMW. Why can't I have one? I do everything, Lauren and Sanjay do nothing. You'll be sorry when I go. It's a shame you are bald.' Looking back over your message, you worry it might come across as aggressive, so you sign off with 'I love you'.

A tiny voice in the back of your head suggests it might be a good idea to leave it until morning, but you ignore it and press 'send'. Tiny voice is going to feel so stupid when you get that massive pay rise.

Forgetting to Delete Your History

Jasminda's laptop is plugged into the projector, but there's a connection problem and she asks if she can use yours instead. You try to think of an excuse, remembering what you looked at last night and realizing with horror that you forgot to delete your history.

There are no problems connecting your computer. A giant version of your desktop appears in front of all seven people in the meeting room, who are perilously close to seeing the unspeakable images you sought out. You hold your nerve.

Jasminda has opened her presentation, and she's going through the slides. There's little danger of her accidentally sharing your search history and everyone finding out you're into videos of people having sex in giant animal costumes. Now she's taking everyone through a series of charts, and there's no way they could know that, less than twenty-four hours ago, you used that same computer to watch a fluffy Dalmatian shagging an oversized badger.

As if in horrible slow motion, you see that Jasminda has forgotten to include a slide and she is going online to look for an image. She opens your browser and begins to type. One of your secret sites appears on autofill. You keep your head down, desperately hoping that no one has noticed. Except … Jasminda accidentally presses return and bingo, there's that video of the Labrador and the giant rabbit.

You try to explain that it's a perfectly normal fetish and thousands are into it, especially in Japan, but the others just stare at you in shock. Guess who will be getting soft toys in the next Secret Santa?

Having a Zoom Meeting with Senior Management

You're presenting to the three most senior people in your company. This needs to go well. So you spend the morning running through your slides and replacing the Fast and Furious DVDs on the shelf behind you with the inspirational memoirs of self-made millionaires.

Then it's time to go, and you send out a polite

reminder. But nothing happens. Five minutes later, the first board member joins, halfway through an argument with their spouse about how to use Zoom. You get a grainy image of the top right quarter of their face, and they look like they're in a corporate remake of *The Blair Witch Project*. Another boss enters with a grainy image that keeps freezing. Why do the richest people in your company spend the least on technology? They must have some money left after all those yachts. The final boss joins the meeting and somehow has a worse connection. If they were any blockier, they'd be Pac-Man.

You begin your presentation, but one of them can't see it, one has accidentally left and the other is frozen in an expression of angry confusion. You wait for them to get sorted and try *again*, barely holding in your anger as the management stare at their laptops as though they've never seen one before. Then one of them has the audacity to say that there's a problem with the connection and they think the fault might be at *your* end.

You lose it, and launch into a rant about how you have mega-super-ultra-fast fibre-optic plus broadband AND a powerful laptop that you had to pay for with your OWN money because you couldn't open Word on your work one without it CRASHING. You explain that the real fault lies with the arrogant idiots who earn thirty times as much as you but are still using dial-up Internet and an Atari ST.

It feels great to let it out, and it doesn't matter that you're being rude, because none of them can hear you. You agree to end the meeting and email the presentation instead.

Calendar Cringe

A Twitter user admitted that he arranged afternoon 'meetings' in the bedroom with his wife while they were both working from home. Unfortunately, he hadn't set his Outlook calendar to private, and all his colleagues could see what he was up to.

Creating an Email Storm

You emerge from a three-hour meeting and you're absolutely fuming. The chocolate biscuits were replaced by horrible, tasteless, organic lumps of sawdust.

```
            Facebook Fail


An Italian priest was conducting
mass over Facebook Live in 2020,
  when he accidentally turned a
 series of filters on. They showed
  him with googly eyes, a wizard's
hat and beard, and a space helmet.
```

You know you should never write an email in anger, but some things are just too important. You compose a note to the office manager, explaining that you know there's a cost-cutting drive on, but decent biscuits should be sacrosanct. If anything, they should get rid of one of those interns who seem to do nothing but look at Instagram all day.

You press send, and your inbox explodes with automated out-of-office replies. Your heart hammers in your chest as you check back over your email. Somehow, you managed to send it to every employee, not just in your office, but in all your company's offices in eighty-four capital cities. Hundreds are replying to ask why you added them, and hundreds more are replying to the replies. Your inbox has become a horrific reply-to-allpocalypse, and so has everyone's inbox.

A global discussion about biscuits has broken out, and it's bringing the company together in a way that no mission statement ever could. The only slight disadvantage is that no one can actually do any work.

All around your of office, people are folding their arms and glaring at you. Your boss wants to see you. One of the interns takes pity on you and makes you a cup of coffee. In your flustered state, you've forgotten what you said about them. It's only as you sip the coffee while being yelled at by your boss that you notice it tastes *just* a bit phlegmier than usual.

Screen Share Cringe

A Twitter user described how she was on the phone to a guy from IT, and decided to Google him to see what he looked like. She had forgotten she was sharing her screen with him at the time.

Installing an Update

Your computer has been nagging you to update for weeks. It wanted you to do it when you were buying some trainers, when watching Netflix and when you were snooping inside your neighbour's house on a property website. Like a child tugging your sleeve and demanding a new Hot Wheels set, it went on and on until you gave in.

One morning before work, you click 'update'.

You're about to have a shower and get some breakfast, so it should have at least half an hour to do whatever it wants to do. You return to find it's only 18 per cent done. And your computer is telling you not to go near until it has finished.

You grab your phone and look through your calendar, desperately trying to calculate when you'll be able to start work. The update jumps to 31 per cent, and you breathe a sigh of relief. The first 18 was obviously the hardest, and it will be plain sailing from here. Then …

Your computer gets stuck on 45 per cent, and you realize it's doing this deliberately. *This is what you get for ignoring me*, it's saying. *I let you watch TV, I let you buy stuff. I even let you look at eye-wateringly unpleasant things when your partner is out, and it's time I was shown some RESPECT.*

It's on 68 per cent when you are meant to be sending a report to your boss. You beg it to go faster, promising you'll never take it for granted again. You wonder if you should email everyone and tell them what's happening, but you suspect that updating when you have less than twenty-four hours to spare is the sort of basic error everyone should know about.

Eventually, your computer stops sulking and lets you use it again. You have to jump straight into a team meeting in which your boss ticks you off for failing to send the report. You want to tell the truth, but you know your computer is listening. You don't want to anger it again, so you take the hit. It's in charge now. It's no longer your computer. You're its human.

Ebook Cringe

A Twitter user admitted they'd bought their elderly mother a Kindle, linked it to their own Amazon account and told her to read whatever she wanted. She went on to download dozens of explicit erotica titles, all of which showed up on her offspring's purchase history.

Cleaning up Your Social Media

You're waiting for a job interview; you're fully prepared. You're ready to repeat words like 'dependable', 'flexible' and 'energetic' until they give in, and you are rewarded with a marginally shorter commute and slightly more money.

You glance through the glass wall and notice

your potential employer is checking their laptop. You panic as you remember something you once heard. Apparently, 90 per cent of companies look at the social media accounts of new applicants. So you get out your phone and open Facebook, frantically untagging yourself from the photo where you're screaming out of the window of a hen-night limousine, and the one where you're pretending to orally pleasure a statue of Ronald MacDonald. The cat photos can stay, except for the one where you admit you're going to be late for work because Simba the cat is asleep on your lap and you don't want to disturb him.

Zoom Shame

A student in the US went viral in 2020 when she used the toilet, on Zoom, in front of her entire class. She realized her mistake mid-stream and turned the camera away.

Most of your status updates are about how much you hate your current job, and how your clients are dicks, so …

🐾 You delete them and replace them with inspirational business quotes like, 'The moment you put a deadline on your dream, it becomes a goal.'

🐾 You change your personal bio from 'I am here to serve cats' to 'I am a talented and hardworking individual with broad skills and experience'.

🐾 You bulk up your profile with stock shots of smiling business people and links to TED talks, and suddenly you've transformed into a motivated professional rather than a train wreck who gets out of bed at noon on Saturdays.

You're about to put your phone away when an old friend shares a photo from ten years ago with the comment, 'Good times'. Uh-oh. It's *that* picture – when you were sick in the taxi queue and the smell was so bad it made the man behind you chuck up over your head.

You delete it, but too late. Your potential employer has seen it. They're staring at their screen and gagging slightly. There's no way back from this. You tell the receptionist to cancel the interview, and try to make a nonchalant exit.

Signing off an Email

You've finished your email, and you take a moment to admire it. You've put all your points across clearly, and you haven't repeated yourself. Now all you have to do is sign it off.

You type 'Kind regards', but what about 'Best regards'? You can't just send someone kind regards when best ones are available. But there are also 'Warm regards', which have got to be better than cold ones. It's all getting too confusing so you think of something else. 'Yours sincerely' is definitely out. You might as well wear a stovepipe hat, smoke a pipe and write, 'Yours respectfully and with great esteem'.

You try 'Take care'. But it sounds too much like a threat, as if you were putting, 'It would be a shame if anything happened to you, wouldn't it?' It's time for something less formal. You type 'Cheers'. Does that work? Or are you trying too hard to be casual, like when you call a plumber 'mate' and talk about football? How about 'Thanks in advance' or 'Looking forward to hearing from you'? Hmm. They both sound very impatient, like you're tapping your fingers on your desk and waiting for them to do some work.

So what's left? A smiley emoji? No, you're not a teenager tweeting a K-pop star. 'Keep up the good work'? Too crawly. 'You always bring a smile to my face'? Too creepy. 'Have a great weekend'? Damn, that would work, but it's only Wednesday. 'You rock'? Eww.

You've spent longer worrying about the sign-off than you did writing the email, and it doesn't look like there'll be a way out anytime soon. You abandon the email and call them instead.

Video Call Fail

Political analyst Robert Kelly went viral in 2017, when his interview with the BBC was interrupted first by his four-year-old daughter, then his nine-month-old son and then his wife, who crawled in and frantically dragged the children out. Few could have guessed how ahead of his time Kelly was, and how we'd all be replaying similar scenes three years later.

Having a Side Hustle

Your office manager has sent an all-staff email, claiming someone has been using company equipment for their personal projects. They would like anyone with information to come forward. Your eyes dart around the room, glancing at the faces of your co-workers. Do any of them suspect you're the guilty one?

We all need a side hustle these days, and using work equipment is fine. But you know you went too far when you printed out three copies of your novel, and the low ink notification came up. You must have left the title page behind by mistake.

You tell yourself to keep your head down. You didn't write it under your real name, and you haven't told anyone about it. But then you wonder why you should be ashamed of your writing. It comes from your heart, so why keep it to yourself?

You reply to all, confessing to printing out the dinosaur erotica. You're confident that *Seduced by the Stegosaurus* will make you a millionaire, and you'll buy the company a hundred new printers as a leaving present when it becomes a bestseller.

There are millions of people out there just

like you, who long for nothing more than to lose themselves in the cold embrace of a T-Rex, or feel the hard, scaly tongue of a randy diplodocus on their naked flesh. It's time for dinophiles like you to stop living with shame.

Your office manager replies that it must be very nice for you, but they are actually looking for the person who's been using padded envelopes for their Etsy business.

Email Shame

In 2011, a London lawyer's email
to his secretary went viral. He
demanded £4 to cover a dry-cleaning
bill after she had spilt tomato
ketchup on his trousers. To make
matters worse, he sent it to her on
the day of her mother's funeral.

Leaving a Voice Message

· · · · · · · · · · · · · · · · · · · ·

You want to pass on some information to a colleague, but they're not answering. You're on your way to a meeting, and don't have time to stop and type. You'll just have to go old-school and leave a voice message.

You manage to get everything you want to say into a quick, clear message. It's a textbook voicemail, except for one thing. You end it by saying 'love you'. It's an easy mistake to make. You only ever send voice messages to your partner, so it's no surprise that it slipped out. But you can't just leave it. You call back and leave a message, explaining that you don't love them. And now you worry that you've been too harsh.

You try again and clarify that while you don't technically love them, you do like them a lot. You try and move on, but now you're wondering if that sounded too much like flirting. So you call back, just to make things crystal clear. You say that you weren't coming on to them, in fact you're very happy in your current relationship. But if you were single, they'd be in the top ten colleagues you'd try.

Picturing your other colleagues, you realize it's still potentially quite insulting, so you call once again and say you've changed your mind. They'd actually be the one you'd ask *first*, as they have great hair and keep themselves in shape. They're incredibly attractive by the standards of your office, and probably by the standards of all the international offices too.

Feeling that you've brilliantly explained yourself, you put your phone back into your pocket and head for the meeting. It's only when you emerge that you get the email. Your colleague has shared all your voice messages with HR, and they want to discuss them 'URGENTLY'.

Facebook Fail

A Facebook user posted 'Jesus makes things so hard for me', prompting a Christian friend to assure her that he moves in mysterious ways and she should keep praying.

She explained that Jesus was actually the name of her fourteen-year-old son, who had just been suspended for punching a janitor.

Sitting Next to Someone Who Doesn't Know How to Use a Computer

• • • • • • • • • • • • • • • • • •

You get it. Not everyone has to be a tech geek. But a new colleague has just taken the desk next to you, and they're terrible with computers. You have no idea how they hold down a job.

It starts when you notice them typing with one finger. They look down at the keyboard and up at the screen again after EVERY SINGLE LETTER. How do they ever get anything done? And they're going through drop-down menus, not using shortcuts. They're even deleting chunks of text *one letter* at a time rather than selecting them. And they seem to be printing everything out and putting it – why, oh WHY? – in a box file.

It's fine. If that's the way they want to work, let them. They're not hurting you, and you'll learn to block out their noisy alerts. But when they call out the IT technician to ask how to write something in italics, they really start getting to you. And they constantly mistreat their computer, refusing to update *anything*, filling up the hard drive and downloading malware, and then complaining when it doesn't work …

You snap. The power cable isn't plugged into their laptop, and they're on 1 per cent battery. In a minute, it'll die and they'll lose the Word document they've been working on for the past three hours without saving. You dash over to plug it in, but can't stop yourself bursting into a rant about their terrible habits. They look upset, and you have let them win. You have revealed yourself to be an Angry Nerd, and every day in the office is going to be awkward now.

You calm down, and send them an email apologizing for your behaviour. But you can't resist including an attachment that reads, 'I'm not really sorry'. It's not like they'll ever be able to open it.

Facebook Cringe

A Facebook user commented 'How far along r u?' on a holiday photo her friend had just uploaded. Her friend replied, 'I'm not pregnant'. No amount of apologizing can get you out of that one.

Realizing You're the Only One Still Working from Home

. . . .

You button a shirt over your pyjama top and attempt to flatten down your hair, just in time for another Zoom catch-up. You click on the link. Straight away, you know something isn't right. The usual scruffy sofas and wonky bookshelves have been replaced with glass walls and potted plants. Wait a moment … is everyone back in the office?

Viral Shame

An educational quiz website for children featured the pop-up message, 'Slow down and make sure your correct!'

The meeting goes on, but you can't focus. You thought everyone was still meant to be working from home. Why are they there? Could it be that they don't want you back? If so, what do you do that annoys them all so much? Your habit of playing the drums on your desk with biros? Never making anyone else a coffee? The stinky cod in parsley sauce you microwave for dinner every day?

You can't let the meeting continue until you know why you've been cast out.

Interrupting your boss, you break down in tears and beg them to take you back. You promise you'll never be late again, that you'll do your timesheets and you'll never steal another stack of Post-its from the stationery cupboard. You just want to come back.

An awkward silence follows, broken only by your

pitiful sobs. Then your boss points out that the plan for returning to the office was detailed at the bottom of an email he sent months ago, and everyone is welcome to come back. And now you remember what the really annoying thing is that you do. You never bother to read emails properly.

SOCIAL
MEDIA

Pressing the Wrong Reaction Button

A vague acquaintance has posted some bad news and everyone else has responded with thoughtful messages. You're not a monster. You can't simply scroll past ... But do you know them well enough for a 'You okay hun?' That's quite a high level of intimacy for someone who worked two desks away from you in 2011.

The answer is simple. You can just click the 'sad' button. Send them a blubbing yellow emoji and sit back, safe in the knowledge that you've given them all the emotional support you could possibly have done. So you click on it, thankful that your quandary is over and you can move on. But you gasp in horror as you realize your unsteady fingers have clicked the 'haha' button by mistake. You change it, but too late. Your acquaintance will have seen. You have become an online Caligula, laughing at the pain of others for your own twisted pleasure. You might as well set fire to some slaves.

Viral Shame

An especially annoying note left on the windscreen of a damaged car went viral in 2017. It read, 'I hit your car and I am pretending to write my info because people are watching me. Hope you can fix it.'

You write an apology, but you're just digging yourself in deeper. The last thing your ex-colleague needs right now is a snivelling response from someone she half-knew a decade ago.

There's nothing else for it. You'll have to delete her as a friend, and pray that you never pass her on the street when she remembers you as the uncaring monster who jeered at her the day her spaniel had leg surgery.

Making Friends with an Annoying Facebooker

You meet someone at a party and they soon send you a friend request. They seemed nice, so you accept.

Scrolling down their timeline, you notice that they share a lot of weird, inspirational memes. While you're sure it's true that the future belongs to those who believe in the beauty of their dream, you're not quite sure what it has to do with a stock shot of a candle.

You soon get a notification that they've tagged you. Perhaps some photos from the party? No, it's an obvious hoax about how Facebook are about to start charging, but if you copy and paste their status, you'll continue to get it for free. You quietly untag yourself.

Twitter Fail

In 2011, UK politician Ed Balls attempted to search for his own name on Twitter, but accidentally tweeted it instead. The tweet went viral, and Ed Balls day is still celebrated every year on the 28th of April. It will probably still be celebrated in 2000 years' time, long after everyone has forgotten who Ed Balls was, or what the Internet was.

It's another cut-and-paste status next. As a test to see who reads their updates, they're demanding that everyone leaves a comment about how they met. You decline.

Their next update informs you that they've just cleaned out their friend list, and congratulates you on still being there as it means you've made the cut. All you've ever done is remove yourself from their posts. What must the people who got deleted have been like?

Then you get a notification that they've commented on one of your posts. You click through and discover that they've left a link to their Etsy store, which offers poor watercolours of dogs. They've crossed the line. You unfriend them.

Three days later, you bump into them in real life, and they're upset.

They ask why you did it, and you want to explain that you had no idea someone who seems so normal in real life could be such an irritant online. But you just pretend it was an accident, promise to add them again, and resign yourself to a future of obvious hoaxes and inspirational quotes.

Email Fail

A college professor shared an unfortunate email sign-off mistake on Twitter. They had meant to write 'stay in touch', but typed 'stay and touch' instead.

Getting No Likes
on Facebook

It's a Monday night and you're watching a band in a giant indoor arena. You're having more fun than everyone else on your friend list, and you need them to know. You spend the first three songs getting the right picture, much to the annoyance of everyone behind you. You post it with the caption, 'Can't believe I got this close to the stage!!!'

You refresh your app, but there are no likes. You post a slightly different photo. Still nothing. Perhaps your friends and relatives don't fully understand how much fun you're having. You post again, checking in at the venue, and spelling out exactly who the artist is and how brilliant it is to watch them.

Your friends still ignore you.

Well this is just great. You dragged yourself all the way out here, you won't be home until after midnight and your so-called friends don't even have the decency to be jealous.

Your partner tells you to put your phone away and enjoy the show, but you can't let it go. You type, 'Listen, I paid £65 plus booking fee, and I queued for twenty minutes for plastic cups of lukewarm lager and horrible red wine, the least you ungrateful bastards can do is give me a "like".' But even this gets nothing. The crowd are stomping and cheering, but you're too annoyed to focus. It's only when you're outside and queuing for a cab that you realize what happened. The coverage inside the venue was so bad that your app wasn't working properly. Your updates actually got plenty of likes, except for that last one.

Not only have you ruined your night for no reason, but you've revealed to all your friends how pathetically desperate for affirmation you are.

Text Fail

A Twitter user shared a text from her mother that read, 'Great news — your grandfather is homosexual!' She had intended to type 'home from hospital', but autocorrect changed it.

Getting into an Online Argument

An interesting topic is trending, so it's time for a quick look at what people are saying before you go to bed.

Oh dear. Someone has said something that's just plain wrong. No doubt they'll be grateful when you point out their mistake. You type your comment, and hope that will be an end to it. Surprisingly, your opponent doesn't accept your valid point. In fact, they're repeating their blatantly incorrect one even more fiercely.

Zoom Fail

A student reported on Twitter that her professor shared her screen during a Zoom class, and everyone could see a folder labelled 'DIVORCE' on her desktop.

You know you're right, so you can't leave it. A quick Google search finds an article that backs you up. As soon as you share this, it will all be over. But your opponent still isn't convinced. They send a link of their own, from a much less reputable source. You explain this to them. They dig in deeper.

Perhaps this is a sign that you and the other person will never see eye to eye. Rather than getting annoyed, you should just celebrate the diversity of opinions in our world. It would be boring if we were all exactly the same. But there's having a different opinion, and there's being factually wrong. And you need to school this fool. You hit them with valid point after valid point, and they repeat their mistaken opinion over and over again.

Finally, they stop. You had the last word, which means you're the winner. A glance at the time reveals it's 2a.m. You'll be groggy tomorrow, but at least you made one person see the error of their ways. If everyone did that, then eventually there would be no more idiots, and everything would be okay again.

You are about to shut down when you spot a notification. The idiot is back. And this time, with a raucous bunch of boneheads.

You make yourself a coffee. This could take some time.

Viral Shame

A picture of a scowling muscleman got a lot of attention in 2019. Not because everyone was terrified by it, but because his mum could clearly be seen in a mirror behind him, taking the photo. Bless.

Becoming a Meme

A photo of you enjoying a night out appears on Facebook. Except that you don't look like you're enjoying yourself. You were pretty tired when it was taken, and didn't have the energy to smile. You don't think anything more about it, until you see it on social media a few weeks later with some unrelated text over the top.

A quick search reveals hundreds of similar versions

of the image. You have been christened 'Disgruntled Lady' and uploaded to a meme generator. People are superimposing ridiculous complaints like 'No fennel at the deli', 'New toaster has no bagel setting' and 'The ironing lady forgot to pick up my clothes again'. You feel like you should complain to someone, but you have no idea who makes memes, or who is in charge of them. You'd only be living up to your disgruntled character anyway.

You're shocked when you start getting recognized on the street, and people stop to ask you for selfies. You instinctively smile, but that's not what they want. None of their friends will recognize you unless you're frowning. Then your boss declares that your fame is distracting everyone, and fires you.

You are forced to make a living appearing in regional nightclubs and recording birthday messages on Cameo. You have to do them in character, of course. But that's not too difficult now. The meme has come true, and you really are Disgruntled Lady. If only you'd smiled when you had the chance.

Launching an Unwise Moral Crusade

You spot an ad for an escort service on a website. It's bad enough that these sordid services exist, without them being allowed to promote themselves. You try and ignore it, but when you chance upon the same vile advert on a different site, you decided to take action. You screenshot the abomination and share it on Twitter. You add people who are likely to share your indignation, sit back and wait for it to blow up.

This could be the moral crusade that makes your name. Imagine if your campaign works. There will be TV appearances, press interviews, maybe some sort of medal. You stare at your tweet, but it just sits there, unnoticed by the world. Finally, a reply. Someone has pointed out that that the ads are individually targeted and based on your browsing history. You feel your cheeks flushing. Well there was that time … You just wanted to look … But you'd never dream of actually …

Zoom Fail

A US college student surprised
his classmates during a Zoom
lesson in 2021. Unaware that
his camera was on, he took
his phone to the barbers and
got a haircut during class.

Now your tweet is getting attention. It's going viral, along with the reply. You are becoming famous, not as a saviour of standards but as a ridiculous hypocrite.

You've been a bad, bad boy. Maybe it's time to give that dominatrix a quick call again.

Mansplaining

A fact floats by on your feed, but it seems wrong. You remember seeing something on TV a few years ago that contradicted it. Perhaps you should reply to the poster, and explain their mistake.

You reply and move on, glad to have shared your knowledge. A few seconds later, the notifications begin. You're getting more angry messages than you can read, and you think back over your recent behaviour, trying to remember if you've dumped any cats in wheelie bins recently.

You scroll up and the full horror of the situation hits you. The person you corrected was the leading expert in the field. She's someone who's dedicated her life to publicizing human understanding, and you're someone who watched the last ten minutes of a documentary while waiting for *Top Gear* to start.

Email Fail

A Twitter user described how she tried to type the phrase 'I'll shoot you an email when I find out', but accidentally pressed send after the first three words.

Worse, she is woman and you are a man, which makes you guilty of mansplaining. You have become one of those chauvinists who begins every sentence with 'actually' and overrules women with wrong answers in pub quizzes. So you delete the tweet, but too late. Someone has screen-grabbed it and it's going viral. The angry replies are spiralling out of control, and you've just had a message of support from Laurence Fox and an invitation to appear as a shit-stirring guest on local radio.

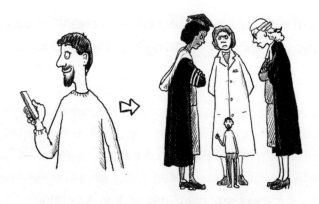

There's no way back now. You'll just have to lean into the toxic masculinity and become one of those four guys in skinny jeans outside a bar. Your new life as a men's rights activist awaits, and there's nothing you can do to stop it.

Phone Disaster

A Twitter user admitted to accidentally dialling her mother during sex. Far from being embarrassed, her mother was actually concerned, as she thought her daughter had hurt herself.

Being out with a Rude Friend who Won't Stop Looking at Their Phone

You're in the middle of telling your friend about a new colleague you dislike when a notification appears on their phone. They stare down at their screen in a trance, and nothing you can say or do can wake them from it. Finally, they look up and you continue your rant. You can't quite remember where you were up to, so you go through all your colleague's bad points again. You have to stop briefly to answer a WhatsApp message, but soon get back into your stride.

Ten minutes later, your friend responds to a text and goes temporarily deaf again. What can be so important that it demands their immediate reply? Nonetheless, you manage to pick up your diatribe again, stopping only to post a quick photo on Instagram.

You're just getting on to the subject of how pathetically your new colleague sucks up to the boss when your friend breaks off again, because of a Facebook notification. You wonder if you should say something. That's the third time they've done this.

You don't want your night out to end in argument, so you leave it and go back to your tirade. You pause a few minutes later to check the Instagram responses, and you hear your friend's chair scraping across the floor. They say that they're leaving because *you've* been staring at your phone for ten minutes, and you shouldn't have invited them out if all you were going to do was stare at a screen.

You're so shocked you can hardly speak. You thought *they* were the guilty one. But, like the twist in a 90s thriller, it turns out you were the real villain all along.

Email Shame

In 2002, a banker at Credit Lyonnais sent an email to five friends in which he boasted he'd been sexually pleasured by a female friend while on the phone to his fiancée. His friends responded by forwarding the email, which went viral and cost him his job. The female friend in question was contacted by the press and denied it was true.

Reacting to the Death of a Celebrity

An old rock star is trending on Twitter, and you wonder if they've died or said something racist. It's the former, and you breathe a sigh of relief. It's OK to still enjoy their songs. But everyone on your socials is in mourning, and you're worried you don't feel upset enough. You never met the star in question. They're one of hundreds of thousands of people you didn't know who died today. But everyone will think you're harsh and uncaring if you don't join in.

But what to post? A link to a YouTube video? A memory of the first time you heard their biggest hit? A self-aggrandizing rant about how they inspired you to achieve your own success? YES! You've got it. You think of a brilliant pun based on one of their songs. You're about to share it when you check Twitter and see that everyone else has had exactly the same thought. Your heart sinks. You're the real victim in all this.

A memory wafts by, bringing with it the scent of incense and Portaloos. Wait. You saw them live. They were on at Glastonbury once. You must have taken a photo. You scramble through your drawer, desperately looking for your old Nokia. You can post the picture, talk about how great the gig was and tag everyone who was there with you. This will be brilliant grieving. You'll totally win social media today.

Selfie Disaster

A model's bathroom selfie went viral
in 2018, but only because of the
bizarre layout of the room. There
was a towel rack behind the toilet,
a plug directly above it and the
toilet roll holder ... miles away
on the other side of the room.

You locate the phone, charge it and scroll through the pictures. You find the one you're after. It's made up of about sixteen pixels, and seems to feature nothing but the backs of some heads and a few flags, but you're sure the tiny figure on the stage is the rock star in question.

You're about to post it when disaster strikes. Your friend has uploaded a selfie of them with the star. Apparently, they met them in a restaurant once. And there's no way you can compete with that. You might as well give up. Now, *finally*, you're as upset as everyone else.

Being in a WhatsApp Group with Someone Annoying

Your WhatsApp group used to be fun. Everyone loved the GIFs you shared and the random conversations you started. But now someone new has joined and it's just not the same.

They spam the group with photos of their garden and kitchen. They post huge chunks of text that you scan through looking for a point. They ask about the opening hours of local shops. You snarkily post a link to Google as your reply, but they don't take the hint. They carry out lengthy two-way chats that should be direct messages, strangling general conversation.

Zoom Disaster

A guest on BBC Wales went viral in 2021, when viewers spotted what appeared to be a sex toy on the shelf behind her. One Twitter user congratulated her on 'keeping up with her DIY'.

People begin to leave, and you message the admin and ask if they can kick the new person out. They say it wouldn't be fair, as they haven't broken any group rules. Your beloved group has been killed by this human knotweed, and there's nothing you can do about it. Then you have an idea. You message the admin again, and suggest starting a new group containing everyone except the annoying new member. That way you'll be able to go on as before without causing upset.

They dismiss your idea, which is a shame. You really thought you'd solved it. It's only a few weeks later that you realize what's happened. Everyone has already moved to a new group. And you weren't invited. It turns out there were two annoying people in the group.

Taking a Personality Quiz

You don't give away your personal information lightly. Years ago, you fell for the old 'pornstar name' trick, which involved adding the name of your first pet to your mother's maiden name, and coming up with a hilarious moniker that answered the two most popular security questions.

You've learned your lesson, and are much warier now. But your friend has just shared a Sorting Hat personality quiz on Facebook, and they've got Gryffindor. You've got to do it, because you've got to see if you get Hufflepuff.

It wants to know your favourite colour. It's yellow. Perfect. This is going well. Next, the name of the street where you grew up. Park Road. Hmm. You're not really sure if that's Hufflepuff, but you answer honestly. You can't trick the Sorting Hat.

Now it wants to know what your first car was. Uh-oh. A VW Polo, and you reckon that's pretty Slytherin. But you soldier on, desperate to get the result you want. The next question is about your bank. Nationwide. Surely, that's got to be Hufflepuff. The following asks for your account number. You type it in, and it looks just right. It's exactly the kind that Cedric Diggory would have. Finally, it wants your sort code, start date and CVV number. They all feel so Hufflepuff, as if Newton Scamander himself were typing them.

You submit your results, and the hat puts you exactly where you wanted to be. You are officially a Hufflepuff. You are also currently buying 200 Amazon gift cards in Shanghai. You post the results online and your friends try to warn you that the test is a scam. They're probably just jealous. Typical Slytherins.

Deliberate Zoom Fail

In 2021, an App called 'Zoom Escaper' was launched. It lets you sabotage your own audio stream, giving you the perfect excuse to leave a dull meeting. You can make your connection sound choppy and broken up, you make your voice echo, and you can add sound effects like a barking dog and a crying baby.

Viral Shame

A passive-aggressive note from an office kitchen went viral in 2015. It asked whoever was putting food in the bin to leave it elsewhere as it was stinking the place out. The guilty party replied 'sorry' — in ketchup.

Humblebragging

A holiday at last. The stress of the flight and checking into the hotel is over and it's time to relax on the beach with a cocktail. You feel the sun on your skin, gaze at the lapping waves and sip the peach and prosecco. It's perfection. Well, almost. There's something missing, but what? Of course! You haven't shared your experience on social media yet.

It doesn't count as enjoyment until everyone else knows about it.

You take a selfie, choosing the filter that best captures your look of smug contentment. It's time to upload it. You type, 'Loving the resort #beach #sunshine #ocean #waves #relaxed #chilling'. No. The tone isn't quite right. You need to humblebrag. You consider, 'Couldn't afford the Dom Perignon so had to settle for the Bellini #beach #sunshine #ocean #waves #relaxed #chilling'. Still not humble enough.

You try again: 'Wish I'd got into better shape for this holiday. Everyone else is so toned #beach #sunshine #ocean #waves #relaxed #chilling'. No. You need to go further. You change it to: 'Oh god this holiday is so perfect and I'm such an idiot. How dare I even look at anyone when they're so brilliant and I'm such a twat? I'm so worthless I should be wearing a lice-ridden hairshirt instead of a bikini and licking the shower plugholes rather than drinking a cocktail.

Stupid, stupid me #beach #sunshine #ocean #waves #relaxed #chilling'.

There. That's better. You post it, and can finally sit back and relax.

Correcting Someone on Their Grammar

You're engaged in a heated discussion on social media. It isn't an argument yet, but it could easily flare into one. And you're trying to resist doing something that will absolutely guarantee that. You want to correct the other person's grammar.

You knew something was up when they used 'literally' for emphasis, rather than for something that's literally true. You managed to move on. That battle has apparently already been lost. Then the grammar mistakes started. 'Its' instead of 'It's'.

'There' instead of 'They're'. 'Your' instead of 'You're'. You could just type an asterisk, followed by the correction. You'd get it off your chest, and they wouldn't get too angry, would they?

TV Fail

A Twitter user described how they paid over £1000 for a 4K TV, as they thought the picture on their HD one was slightly blurry. The next day they found out they needed new glasses.

But what if they're dyslexic? That wouldn't look great. On the other hand, they could just be lazy. They could just be the sort of person who can't be bothered to learn a few simple rules of their own language. And now things are getting worse. They're throwing in random commas, using emoji instead of full stops and have even used two adjacent full stops, which was possibly meant to be an ellipsis. But when they use 'could of' instead of 'could have', you've got to wade in.

Email Fail

A Twitter user described how they sent an angry response to someone who spelt their name wrong in an email reply. They said their name was important to them, and it wasn't difficult to get it right. Then they looked back at their original email and realized they were the one who'd spelt it wrong in the first place.

You type, 'If you want to have a serious discussion, you need to work on you're grammar'. You press return, and then the extent of your error sinks in. You try to type '*your', but three other people have beaten you to it. After all, what could be more fun than correcting a pedant? You need to walk away *now*. There's no coming back from this. If only you could of checked what you'd written.

Getting Caught up in a Facebook Prank War

You have a hundred notifications on Facebook, and you're worried that something has happened. But it turns out the new guy in the office is just pranking you. He's gone through all your recent photos and reacted with the laughter emoji.

You smile, but you *don't* forget. A week later, you send him a birthday message, even though you know you're a month early. Dozens of his friends comment, apologizing for forgetting it, and asking why they haven't been invited to the celebrations.

He takes it to the next level, tagging you in photos of people outside pubs who have passed out and are covered in vomit.

Password Fail

According to a study carried out in 2020, over 2.5 million people use '123456' as their password.

Your move. An opportunity presents itself when they leave their laptop unguarded and logged into Facebook. Of course, you could post 'Just had a really lovely shit', but that stuff is for amateurs. What you actually do is change their privacy setting so they are the only person who can see their posts. You giggle from behind your hands for a couple of days as they wonder why no one is reacting to their updates.

They try to laugh when you reveal your practical joke, but you can tell you've got to them. You apologize and agree on a truce. Except ... a week later, you absent-mindedly pat your trouser pocket in the office kitchen. Your phone is missing. You race back to your desk and find it exactly where you left it. But your enemy is smirking.

When you open the Facebook app, you discover

that the default language has been set to Mandarin, and you've sent hundreds of friend requests to the 'people you may know' list. You change the language back and delete the post that claims you've just got engaged to someone from your school. You spend the rest of the day explaining what happened to your relatives and apologizing to the fifty random friends who were deleted.

You need to step away from the battle, because there's only one way this is going to end. They'll leave their laptop unattended again, and you'll announce their death and change their page to a memorial.

Having a Digital Detox

You're going to do it. You're actually going to switch your phone off. You're going to leave it in your car and go for a walk. You examine the phone. Is it bad that you've had it for two years and haven't worked out how to turn it off yet? Never mind. You toss it into the glove compartment, lock the car and set off. It feels like you've lost a limb, but you tell yourself you'll get used to it.

Mansplaining Fail

When Katie Mack shared her concerns about climate change, a male Twitter user suggested she should go away and learn some actual science. She pointed out that she already had a PhD in astrophysics, and anything more would be overkill.

You're alone with your thoughts. The problem is that your thoughts are all about what's happening online. You probably shouldn't have announced this on Facebook, because now you're wondering how everyone is reacting.

You reach the top of a hill and the sun emerges from behind a cloud, filling the valley below with soft, Instagrammable light. You find yourself miming taking a photo. It's a reflex action you can't control. You wonder what's wrong with your ears, and then you realize that there's no podcast in them. All you're left with is the sound of birdsong and distant church bells, which are adding nothing to your knowledge of popular culture. You keep going, but the withdrawal symptoms get worse. You find yourself asking a tree what it thinks about Billie Eilish, and describing an avocado and quinoa salad to a squirrel.

Your lack of connection becomes too much to bear, and you collapse to the ground, grimacing in pain. A concerned onlooker rushes over to see if you're okay. You ask to borrow their phone, and they assume you need to make an emergency call. But when they hand it over, all you actually do is check what's trending on Twitter. Apparently, a new iOS update has been released, Taylor Swift has dropped a surprise track and a TV star from the '80s has been cancelled.

It isn't much of a digital fix, but it's enough to get you back on your feet. You hobble to your car, desperate to get a proper dose of internet and restore yourself.

Netflix Fail

A Twitter user described how they kept using their ex's Netflix account after they'd broken up, as they didn't want to pay for their own. Their ex let them watch almost the entire run of a TV show, then changed their password before they could watch the last episode.

Doomscrolling

Real life has become a bleak dystopia and you can't turn away. Every time you glance at your phone, something terrible has happened and everyone on social media is explaining why you should feel even worse about it than you already do. If you're ever close to feeling contentment or calm, you'll ruin it for yourself by glancing at a news app and setting off another wave of worry.

Happily lying in your back garden and watching clouds? Why not follow some breaking news about a natural disaster? Out for a lovely meal with your partner? Why not browse an article speculating on what the next pandemic will be? Lost in a good book?

Why not ruin it with some downbeat predictions about what life will be like a decade from now?

Take a step back, and it's easy to see what's going on. Humans are hard-wired to seek out bad news. Being aware of danger helped our distant ancestors survive and they passed the trait on to us. But at least they didn't have to spend all night reading scaremongering opinion pieces about sabre-toothed cats once they'd escaped them.

You decide to override your programming and seek out good news instead. A fifty-year-old accountant has become a viral dance sensation. A 100-year-old man has completed a marathon. A five-year-old girl has raised hundreds for charity with her inspirational paintings of rainbows.

It turns out that uplifting stories are even worse than depressing ones. They just remind you that everyone else has done amazing things while you've been gloomily staring at your phone. Anyway, something that sounds worrying is trending on Twitter. It could a new apocalyptic computer game, or something happening in real life. Better check.

Zoom Fail

A Twitter user confessed that she accidentally burped during a Zoom meeting. Because of the noise, she became the main image on speaker view, so she couldn't even deny it was her.

Getting Used to a New Facebook Layout

Facebook has changed its layout, and your brain can't cope. They've shifted the main feed to the right, added some confusing new icons, and made the advert bar slightly wider.

You fiddle around in the settings and find an option that takes you back to the old layout. Offended by your choice, Facebook asks why you're reverting, and you fill the textbox with an angry diatribe about how they've ruined everything.

Facebook Fail

When police returned a woman's stolen phone to her, she found that the thief was still logged into the Facebook app. She took the opportunity to tell all his friends what he'd done.

Facebook soon announces that the new layout is about to become mandatory, and you lose your shit. You post an update, threatening to leave if it happens. Mark Zuckerberg doesn't even bother to comment. You join a brave, underground resistance in the form of a group demanding to keep the old layout, but Big Tech ignores the little guy and pushes the changes through anyway. So you stay true to your word, and abandon Facebook but … You open it again, thirty minutes later, because you're bored of Twitter and Instagram.

But you're still angry that they had to change things. Why couldn't they just leave them as they were? Then a vision of 2009 Facebook floods into your mind. It's like looking at cuneiform on ancient stone. People are writing on your wall. The only reaction button is a 'like'. You are poking someone, and they are poking you back. A friend has lost their mobile and created a group so they can get everyone's number again. Someone has changed their relationship status to 'It's complicated'. Someone has invited you to play Farmville. You have taken a personality test that automatically posts the result on your wall. Your friend has been hacked, and is spamming you with links to a weight loss pill.

You remember that you've complained every time they've changed Facebook, and have to admit that maybe, just maybe, progress can be a good thing.

SatNav Fail

In 2013, a Belgian woman programmed her SatNav to take her to a train station 38 miles away. However, the faulty device led her on a series of disastrous wrong turns, and she ended up 900 miles away in Zagreb, Croatia.

Being Stuck in a Terrible WhatsApp Group

You let out a weary sigh as a notification from your least favourite WhatsApp group appears. It's called 'Eggsy's Stag Do Banter' after a trip to Barcelona you took five years ago, and you've been unable to escape it ever since.

Shit Dave has posted a picture of a queue outside Home Bargains and commented that he's confused because he can't see you in it. According to the lore of the group, you're the tight one because you vetoed going to Vegas. You reply with the obligatory cry-laughing emoji.

Eggsy is the oldest in the group, although only by a matter of months, so everyone adds a comment about him joining the queue for a Zimmer frame and some incontinence pads. Greggs is the fattest member, or at least he was the last time you all met in real life, so you pretend he's heard that donuts are half price, and he's going to queue as well. There.

Banter done. You can go now.

Except ... Greggs has linked to a YouTube clip of someone driving a McLaren out of a dealership and crashing straight into a wall, with the caption 'Shit Dave takes a test drive'. You respond with the laughter emoji and are about to comment that it was really Eggsy and his bifocals fell off, but you can't bring yourself to. Instead, you type, 'Guys, please can we stop this now? We've been doing the same jokes for five years. It's getting really old.'

Facebook Shame

A Facebook prankster claimed that if you type your password as a comment, it will automatically convert to asterisks when you press 'share' as a security feature. He added 'My password is ********' as an example. A few of his friends fell for it, and no doubt had to spent the rest of their day resetting their passwords.

For a moment, nobody responds. Perhaps you've finally made them see sense and the group can be abandoned. Greggs responds that at least it will never get as old as Eggsy. Eggsy responds by saying that at least he isn't so fat that he needs his own postcode. And everyone responds with laughing emojis. You are trapped in the bants forever.

Celebrating Your Birthday on Facebook

You're woken up by your partner with a surprise breakfast, and a gift that's exactly what you wanted. You take a picture of both and open Facebook so you can upload it. But you have no notifications. Odd. There are usually a few early birds who've sent birthday messages by now. You decide against uploading the photo. You can't be the first person to mention that it's your birthday on Facebook. That's practically begging.

At work, everyone takes a mid-afternoon break to give you a cake and a card. It's all going well until you check Facebook and see that you still have no messages. What's going on? Is this the year that everyone is admitting they never actually liked you?

After work, your partner takes you out for a meal at your favourite restaurant. You can order whatever you want on your special day, but you can't stop thinking about Facebook. By now your phone is usually buzzing with acquaintances writing 'Many happy returns' and 'Have a good one'. But your phone hasn't been this dead since your last long-haul flight. Your rare steak tastes like ashes in your mouth as you wonder what's happened to all the cakes, balloons and gift emojis.

Text Fail

A Twitter user contacted a girl to ask for a second date, adding, 'I can't wait to see those big beautiful dimples of yours'. Unfortunately, autocorrect changed 'dimples' to 'nipples'.

Your partner asks if something is up. You usually share everything, but you couldn't possibly explain this. In bed, later that night, you can't bring yourself to do anything but refresh your phone. What have you done to make everyone hate you? Did you post something offensive and get cancelled without realizing?

At 11.59p.m. you finally remember. You changed all your personal information, including your date of birth, to private earlier in the year, meaning that none of your friends got the notification that it was your birthday. It turns out they don't hate you after all. Breathing a sigh of relief, you can finally relax and enjoy your birthday.

The clock switches over to midnight. Oh well, at least you had an enjoyable birthday for ten seconds.

Flouncing off Facebook

You're done with Facebook. You want to get back to the real world and live life to the full, just like you did in the days before social media. Instead of getting caught up in the mundane details of other people's lives, you'll be completing triathlons, speaking Spanish and playing the cello. And probably doing them all on a beach at sunset.

You compose a lengthy rant about why you can't stay on the social platform any longer, tagging everyone you count as a real friend and making vague and aggressive comments about how you've encountered 'too much negativity'. You delete yourself and step out into a new world of endless possibility.

Text Fail

A Twitter user revealed he had texted his friend to warn that his girlfriend was coming along that night, so it would be better if he didn't share 'certain stories'. But he accidentally sent the text to his girlfriend too.

The problems begin when you go to the gym the next day and find that it's closed due to a power failure. Apparently, the gym made the announcement on its Facebook page. And when you drop your child at the school gates, you discover they're the only one without a packed lunch. The teacher asks if you missed the news about the kitchen being closed, which they shared on their Facebook group. Later that week, you're attacked by a stray Rottweiler while putting the bins out. Its owner explains that it had warned everyone on the local group that the dog was in a very bitey mood, and that no one should approach it. Perhaps cutting yourself off from Facebook wasn't totally practical. But you can't go back after making such a big announcement.

Zoom Shame

In 2021, the Mayor of Antwerp appeared in an interview wearing a smart shirt. He seemed surprised when the interviewer asked why we was just wearing underpants on his bottom half, before realizing that an unfortunately placed mirror behind him had given the game away.

You try borrowing your partner's account to check for important announcements. But you find yourself constantly commenting, and having to explain who you are. In the end, you just reactivate your account. You go back on and delete your post about leaving. You compose an equally dramatic one about re-joining, and the comments are split between supportive messages from your close friends, and from everyone else GIFs of Barack Obama, Joey Tribbiani and Alan Partridge shrugging.

LEISURE

Taking a Bathroom Selfie

Getting ready to go out, you glance in the mirror and can't help noticing how gorgeous you are. It would be a shame to keep such perfection to yourself, so it's time for a selfie. You arrange your hair and then tactically rearrange a few strands to make things look spontaneous. Then you lift your camera high to make your eyes look large and cute, stretch out your neck and turn your face slightly away from the lens. Finally, you suck your cheeks in for the classic 'duck face' pose.

Email Fail

In 2016, a test email was accidentally sent to everyone in the English NHS, which was over 840,000 people. It generated a gigantic email storm, as thousands of people replied to complain, and thousands more replied to the replies.

You take eighteen shots and set about choosing a favourite. After ten minutes of careful deliberation, you post the best. But just as you're about to leave the house your phone begins to buzz. Your friends are telling you that your selfie is being shared. That's got to be a good thing, right? But they don't seem to be congratulating you. One message reads, 'I think you'd better see this ...' You click the link.

Emoji Fail

A Twitter user revealed that her mother had sent her news that the family dog had died, followed by the crying with laughter emoji. She thought it was the one you used when you were sad.

There's your selfie, but there's a white circle around something behind you. You were too busy gazing at your own face to check back there. The colour drains from your face as you realize that your toilet has been highlighted. Now it's not as though you didn't flush, but you have a high fibre diet and these days it takes a few tries.

You try to convince yourself that the offending floater is proof of your healthy eating habits, and is nothing to be ashamed of. But the truth is, you ARE mortified. There'll be no coming back from this one. Delete the photo, delete your social media accounts, destroy your laptop, throw your phone in the sea and wear a fake beard for the rest of your life, so no one recognizes you as the 'turd selfie girl'.

Selecting the 'Leave With a Neighbour' Option

You've been waiting over a week for your salted caramel chocolates. You chose the cheapest delivery but, even so, they should be here by now. Talking to the woman next door about the bin collection, you catch a scent on her breath. It takes you a moment to place it, then you realize it's only salted bloody caramel. Like the end of a particularly satisfying episode of *Poirot*, everything slots into place. You clicked on the 'leave with a neighbour' option. You were out when it arrived, it was left next door and she gobbled the whole lot down. Perhaps she's been stealing *all* your deliveries. You still haven't seen any sign of that black coat you ordered either.

Time for revenge. A pranking website is offering spring-loaded glitter bombs that look like ordinary parcels. You'll get one delivered to your house, pretend you're out when it arrives and listen through the wall for the sound of your neighbour swearing as her house is blitzed with glitter.

You're about to get into your car a few days later when you see something that makes your blood run cold. The woman from next door is leaving her house with a black coat on, and it's identical to the one you ordered. If she's going to steal, she could at least be discreet.

Facebook Cringe

A Facebook user called Justin posted that his mother had just caught him masturbating. His friend Andres admitted that the same thing had happened to him, adding 'It's even worse when it's gay porn.' Justin then revealed that his account had been hacked and the incident hadn't really taken place. Andres unconvincingly claimed the same.

You rush over, grab her wrist and announce that you're performing a citizen's arrest. She claims to have no idea what you mean, so you detail her crimes. Then something strange happens. Your neighbour from the other side approaches with the parcels containing your chocolates and jacket. He apologizes for not finding you sooner. You know you should explain things to the woman you've just arrested, but you're in a state of confusion and can't find the words.

A delivery van arrives and drops off a parcel for you. Not sure what else to do, you open it. You remember a second too late. Glitter time.

Reading an Ebook

Technology has killed our attention spans. Where once we'd have passed the winter evenings working our way through *Clarissa* or *Á la recherche du temps perdu*, we now scroll past endless Kardashian selfies and TikTok cats.

Well, that's all going to change. You're going to entertain yourself like everyone did in the old days before they were stupid. And you've chosen one of the greatest content providers of all, Jane Austen. You open your ebook app and get started. 'It is a truth universally acknowledged', etc. This is quality stuff. Elizabeth Bennet is better company than any influencer, and you're really getting into it.

Email Fail

In 2015, a Scottish Twitter user revealed she had attached Jamie Oliver's recipe for chilli beef instead of her CV when applying for a new job. She only realized her mistake when her prospective employers thanked her for the recipe.

Mr Collins has proposed to Elizabeth, but she's swiped right. No, wait. You've opened Tinder and you're getting muddled. Stay focused. Anyway, she doesn't want to marry Mr Collins because he's an idiot. He tags Lady Catherine de Bourgh in everything he posts, just because she's got a blue tick. He's so desperate to get verified. No, hang on. You've opened Twitter. Get back to the story.

Lydia Bennet has just posted another bonnet unboxing video and is about to give a satin bow tutorial. Wait, no. You've gone on YouTube. Now Elizabeth has met Mr Darcy and is posting some insulting GIFs about him in your group, but you kind of ship them. No, you've switched to WhatsApp. It's no use. Your attention span has been shot by years of app addiction, and you'll never be lost in a good book again.

You're about to give up, when you post your

progress via Goodreads and get five likes. You decide to go back to the ebook app. It can't be that much of a waste of time if you're getting likes. Besides, it looks like Mr Wickham is about to get cancelled.

Proving You're Not a Robot

You're about to pay for an online purchase when the site demands proof that you're not a robot. Some sites only require you to tick a box, which doesn't seem like the sort of thing that could fox something clever enough to explore Mars and beat Gary Kasparov at chess, but at least it's easy. Others require you to squint at and retype some blurry, overlapping letters, designed to foil both evil robots and people who can't find their glasses.

This one, however, is different. You have to look at a picture of road with a grid laid over the top, and click on the squares that contain traffic lights. It sounds simple enough, so you give it a go. You fail. The site gives you another chance, asking you to click on squares that contain bridges. Now you're overthinking it, and can't work out if some of them are roads or road bridges. Another fail.

Email Shame

In 2001, an American banker was fired when a boastful email sent from his work address went viral. He claimed he was going to 'fuck every hot chick in Korea' and was already '5 down'. Perhaps most offensively of all, he signed off his email with 'Laters'.

You get another shot. This time you're tasked with clicking on squares that have trees in. Come on. You must be able to do this. You know what a tree is, don't you? But some of them look more like hedges, and you begin to doubt your own judgement. You try your best, but get it wrong again.

These tests are meant to stop robots, and you're getting them wrong. It's time to face facts. You must be a robot. Think about it. You've always had a soft spot for Daft Punk, and you do pretty well at the numbers slot in TV quizzes. Maybe all those memories you think belong to you were actually installed when you were created.

You want to do something to prove to yourself that you're not a robot. You fetch a mallet and attempt to smash your laptop. But you can't do it. Something in your programming forbids it. You failed the online tests, and now you've failed your own test. There's nothing left for you to do but to get chased across some futuristic rooftops by Harrison Ford and deactivate yourself. All those moments will be lost in time like tears in the rain.

Facebook Fail

A teenage boy earned the respect of his friends when he uploaded a Facebook profile picture that showed him standing next to a girl at a posh party. His credibility was dented when the girl in question commented, gently, 'Would really appreciate if you cropped me *out* of this photo, thanks.'

Googling Old Friends

A name pops into your head from nowhere. You realize it was an old school friend, and vague memories come back. He was the one who used to turn the lights on and off, and shout 'disco' whenever the teacher left the class unattended.

You decide to Google him. It will be quite funny to see a middle-aged version of his face staring out from the 'meet our team' section of a supermarket's website. But the first thing that comes up is a TED talk. You suppose it's not surprising that lots of people have the same name, and are about to give up when you realize the face in the thumbnail image looks familiar.

You click on the video. Oh god, it's really him. The same voice. Except that, instead of asking you to pull his finger, he's telling a massive crowd how to keep a workforce happy and motivated.

Zoom Fail

In 2020, a student on Reddit described how she fell asleep during a Zoom class and woke up to find that her parrot had disrupted the entire lesson. It had repeatedly asked the question, 'What are you doing?'

You halt this nightmarish vision, but other names are coming back and you can't stop yourself from finding out about them too. The girl who could burp the alphabet runs a high-end fashion company. The boy who gave you a wedgie in PE is a charity CEO. The boy who drew a Tippex penis on your exercise book has just been given an MBE. How are you suddenly living on a dystopian timeline where everyone became much more successful than you? You used to beat them in exams. How can they be beating you in life? Surely some of your old classmates must have screwed up?

Finally, one of comes through for you. An old geography classmate has been fined for damaging wing mirrors while drunk. Maybe it's time to reconnect on Facebook. If you've learnt anything since leaving school, it's that the secret to happiness is to surround yourself with less successful people. Maybe they'll let you do a TED talk about that.

Drunk Online Shopping

You wake up at two in the afternoon. Your head is pounding, and you vow never to give in to peer pressure and drink gin again. There's a niggling feeling in the back of your mind that you did something stupid last night, but a quick glance reveals you didn't bring home someone who looks like Winston Churchill again.

The doorbell goes and your heart races. The police? Did you assault an officer when they tried to stop you urinating on a roundabout? You rush to the door, only to be greeted by a parcel. Inside is a sixteen-piece gold-effect cutlery set. A thoughtful gift. But who could it possibly be from? Then you realize. It's from you. Rather than passing out on the hallway rug like a normal person, you decided to shop. Now that shops are virtual and always open, you can be two things that end in '-aholic' at once.

Another ring of the doorbell brings an inflatable poo emoji. The next brings a life-sized cut-out of Nicholas Cage. A third brings 100 cushion covers with the same sloth picture, as you got confused on the checkout page.

Twitter Fail

In 2014, a Twitter user asked Donald Trump if he'd retweet a picture of his parents, who had always cited him as a big inspiration. Trump obliged, without realizing that the picture was actually of notorious serial killers Fred and Rose West.

What do these seemingly random objects reveal about your soul? And why is the drunk you so much better at remembering passwords than sober you?

You know you should check your banking app and look at the damage, but you decide to get some more rest instead. You'll be glad you had it tomorrow, when it will become apparent that you also adopted a gigantic Doberman with bowel issues.

Meeting an Online Friend in Real Life

Someone approaches you on the street and you squint at them in confusion. Who on earth could they be? Then you realize. This is one of your online friends, and you're finally meeting in reality.

You had plenty of mutual friends, so you sent them a request, and ever since you've been commenting on each other's posts. You always hoped you'd meet them one day, and now it's happened. So you ask them how you are, and they say they're fine. You say you're fine too.

It's much harder to talk when there isn't a post to comment on, so you remind them of a video of a talking dog you both liked yesterday. You agree that it was pretty cool. A few seconds of silence pass. Your friend asks if you've been busy and you want to respond with a GIF of a cat tapping frantically away on a keyboard, but you remember you can't use GIFs in real life, so you say 'yeah'. Your friend says they are busy too, and smiles, though you can tell they're itching to use an emoji.

Email Disaster

A Twitter user admitted they'd accidentally sent a porn link to a co-worker. In an effort to save face, he emailed the same link to all his other co-workers and pretended it was a virus. A textbook example of digging yourself in deeper.

Crickets are chirping. A church bell tolls in the far distance. A tumbleweed blows into view.

You say you'd better let them go, but it's been great to finally meet them. They agree, and say they hope to see you soon. And as soon as you're out of sight, you get your phone out and message them about how brilliant it was that you ran into each other. They respond with a GIF of Ross Geller saying, 'I know!' Now you're safely apart, the conversation can start to flow.

Appearing in a Stock Shot

One of your old friends is setting up as a photographer, and they want you to be a model. Once you've established that this isn't a creepy chat-up line, you feel flattered to be asked. Maybe it was the career you were meant to have all along.

Your friend will be selling the shots to a stock library, so you'll only get a one-off fee and have no control over how the image is used, but you don't mind. It's not like you've got a million other modelling offers to choose from.

The session goes well, and you hope the shots get used for something. Preferably a huge poster right outside your ex's flat. Three months later, you spot yourself on a website. The good news is that they've chosen a photo in which you look pretty good. The bad news is that they've used it in an ad for incontinence pads.

Email Disaster

In 2008, the HR manager of a US media company emailed other senior managers about an upcoming round of redundancies. He described the plan ... how they'd break the news gently to staff. But he accidentally sent the message to everyone in the company. So much for breaking it gently.

Oh well. Who even looks at online ads, anyway? That's probably the last you'll hear of it. But ... hundreds of messages. It turns out everyone you've ever known looks at online ads. Several friends mention how brave you are speaking out about your problem, and your aunt asks if you can get her a discount. You try and explain the whole stock-shot thing, but no one understands.

The campaign works so well that it extends into outdoor advertising. Just as you'd hoped, a poster of your face goes up outside your ex's flat. He posts it on Twitter along with a cry-laughing emoji. Then, eventually, the ad disappears.

You've just managed to put the whole sorry episode behind you when the photographer messages you with the news that another image from your session is going to be used. You ask if it's another incontinence ad, but he assures you it isn't. It's for pubic lice cream.

Zoom Fail

In 2020, a US college student went viral for forgetting to turn his screen off before rolling a joint in a Zoom class.

Taking Part in a Family Zoom Quiz

Thanks to modern technology, you don't have to wait until Boxing Day to argue about who played James Bond the most times. And unlike Trivial Pursuit, you can't even claim you lost because everyone else got easier questions.

Your parents won last time, so they're hosting tonight. Your dad kicks things off with a round on military tactics in the Second World War, which he regards as ridiculously easy, but everyone scores zero. Next, your mum has come up with a round about everyone in your family. Not only do you suffer the humiliation of losing, but you reveal how little you've actually been listening to anyone for the past few decades.

A multiple-choice round on geography is next, and you score less than the 33.3 per cent you'd have got if you picked options at random. Sport next, and you should be fine with that. Except that the answers aren't quite coming into your mind. You angle your camera up, and stare into the distance with a look of earnest concentration on your face whilst secretly Googling the score of the last FA Cup final. It doesn't count as cheating, because you definitely know the answer. You just can't quite think of it right now.

Your sly Googling technique serves you well in the rounds about television, music and food. Your mum announces that she wants to do a picture round to finish. Google won't be able to help you with that, but you're confident you've built up enough of a lead for victory.

SatNav Fail

In 2008, a driver got his car transporter stuck on the narrow road leading to Gibraltar Point nature reserve in Lincolnshire. It turned out he had intended to drive to Gibraltar, which is 1,600 miles away.

Your mum can't work out how to share her screen, so she emails you the picture round instead. You open the document and share yours. Your brother-in-law's eyes narrow as he peers at his laptop. He asks why the tabs on your web browser are all related to the most recent quiz topics.

The best thing to do now would be admit what you've done, apologize and promise never to do it again. Instead, you pretend you've got connection problems, end the Zoom meeting and try to forget it. Judging by how easily you forgot last year's FA Cup final, that shouldn't be a problem.

Falling for Clickbait

You spot a link to an article about what a famous actress from the '80s looks like now. It claims the result will shock you, so you click on it, navigate your way around the ads and accept all cookies. Twelve clicks later, you finally see the picture. They look pretty much the same, except three decades older. Yet you are shocked, in a way. Shocked that you fell for such crappy clickbait.

You promise you'll never look at anything like it again, but a few days later you spot an article that promises to reveal the surprising reason you're putting on weight. You've noticed your clothes getting a little tighter recently, so you can't resist reading it. The article is written in the form of thirty slides, and at the end it's revealed that you might be eating too much and exercising too little.

Email Shame

In 2005, two secretaries were fired from a Sydney law firm after their email spat went viral. It began with a row about a stolen ham sandwich and soon escalated into personal insults and boasting, with one claiming to earn more money, and the other calling her 'Miss Can't-Keep-a-Boyfriend.'

You tell yourself that you're done with it, but you soon notice an article that asks if NASA have just found proof of alien life. You try to resist, but what if it turns out to be true and you're the first person to share it on your WhatsApp group? You'd be a hero.

It isn't true, of course. How can you stop yourself

getting taken in by this nonsense? Maybe you should think about it in terms you'll understand: you click on a link that claims to lead to an interesting article. You won't believe what happens next!

Will you ever realize that if a headline is written in the form of a question, the answer is 'NO'?

Ten reasons why you should stop being a gullible prick and clicking things like this – 'Number 7 will blow your mind!!!!'

Getting a New Phone

Your colleague has just bought the updated version of your phone and they can't stop showing it off. It's 5 per cent thinner and 3 per cent lighter.

Your old, fat, heavy phone makes you feel like a Neanderthal. You should be using it to fashion rocks into primitive tools, not to check Instagram. Your colleague's phone has a new chip inside that's twice as fast as yours. Just think how much more efficiently you could be scrolling through spam emails about cryptocurrency with that. The phone comes in a specially invented new shade of blue. It looks a lot like regular blue, and though obscured by a cover it only increases your desire. If you can wait just a few months, the price will plummet. But it's no use. You've got to have it now.

You drive to the shop and are stuffing your credit card into the pay machine before the sales assistant has even started their pitch. You emerge, cradling the box like a newborn, and drive home slowly, worried that any sudden jolts might upset it. Inside, you toss aside the hundreds of old phones in your desk drawer, find a pair of scissors and delicately remove the cellophane.

You open the box and peel away the protective

plastic. You turn your phone on and check out the display. You immediately see the problem. It's so perfect you'll *never* be able to use it. How could the trivial details of your humdrum life ever be worthy of such perfection?

Zoom Fail

A group of seven-year-olds went viral in the US when their teacher accidentally left a Zoom call, leaving them unsure what to do. One of them said that if they didn't behave, they'd 'be toast'. They then spent the rest of the time discussing toast.

With trembling hands, you download your favourite apps and sign in. Then Twitter brings the news that a newer, 6 per cent thinner and 4 per cent lighter model of the same phone is coming out next month. And suddenly your new phone looks like something Alan Turing might have designed to win the Second World War. Oh well, at least you won't be afraid to use it now.

Falling Down a Conspiracy Rabbit Hole

A school friend shares a link to a video called 'The Shocking Truth the Mainstream Media Won't Tell You'. You have an open mind, so you watch and are alarmed to discover that Bill Gates is secretly controlling our minds through 5G signals.

You find yourself still pondering it at three in the morning. Suddenly, it all clicks into place. This thing goes deeper than Gates. Piecing together the facts in the way that only someone who has seen through the lies of our lizard rulers could, you concoct an elaborate theory involving Princess Diana, the Illuminati and BTS.

Email Fail

A Twitter user described how she tried to sign off an email with 'thank you so much', but autocorrect changed it to 'thank you douche', and she sent it before realizing.

Risking your life in a brave attempt to wake up the sheeple, you explain everything in a frantic YouTube video. But the Rothschilds and Big Tech join forces to stifle your efforts, meaning you only get four views and a comment from your mum asking if you're okay.

You retreat to your shed, pull out your fillings and curl into a ball to protect yourself from chemtrails.

Surviving on a diet of protein shakes and squirrels, you come to realize that the only way to expose the lies of the secret elite is to destroy every 5G mast in the world. You emerge with a flaming torch and set about your quest.

Luckily, you soon realize the whole thing is bollocks of the highest order, and all you really needed was some fresh air.

Relaxing with Netflix

After a tough day at work, it's time to switch off and relax with a streaming service. But there are so many options confronting you, it feels like the hard graft is only beginning.

There are hundreds of critically acclaimed shows, each hundreds of hours long, and everyone expects you to have watched them all. When did the simple act of watching telly turn into gruelling homework? You haven't got the energy for that, so it will have to be a film. You scroll past rows of possibilities. There are action movies, romantic comedies and a guilt-inducing list of titles you've watched and given up on, reminding you that even passively staring at a glowing rectangle is sometimes beyond you.

Cats comes up on a list of films Netflix that thinks you'd like, which means the streaming giant is accusing you of having a fetish for weirdly sexualized CG creatures that actually look more like possessed monkeys than cats. You'd never have let the assistant from the video shop get away with that.

Flustered by your inability to make a decision, you pick something at random and hope for the best. But the production logos go on so long that clicker's remorse sets in. You can just tell this is going to be one of those studio films where the dialogue seems to have been generated by Google Translate, and the effects sequences look like PlayStation cut scenes.

Back into the menus for more scrolling. Maybe you should try another streaming app? Or perhaps get that box of DVDs out from under the bed? It's not like *Jurassic Park* or *Back to the Future* have ever let you down.

A glance at the clock reveals that it's already bedtime. Movie night has been and gone without a single frame of movie. Your leisure time is over, and it's been even more exhausting than work.

Humblebrag Fail

A woman announced on Facebook she was about to leave for Paris and wanted 'recommendations on the weather'. A snarky friend replied that Google could provide her with the answers, but it wouldn't brag to her friends about her foreign holiday. We know the real reason you post this stuff, people.

Using Your Phone as a Phone

You've read the FAQs, you've tried emailing, and you've had no luck with the chat window. There's no alternative. You're going to have to use your phone to actually phone someone. You hate to do this. Nobody uses phones to call anymore. Why don't you smash up some computers while you're at it, you pathetic Luddite?

You dial the number, and navigate a series of options. None of them seem relevant, but you jab randomly away, as if playing a branching video game where the final reward is a chat with a bored woman in Middlesbrough.

You escape from the option-choosing dungeon and are put on hold *again* due to 'exceptional demand'. You are subjected to some smooth jazz, and you deserve to be. Instead of sorting out your problem online like any normal grown-up, you ran crying to the nearest helpline like it was the '90s.

The minutes roll by. It's costing you more to listen to this music than if you'd bought a deluxe vinyl reissue. You want to give up, but you can't. You've invested too much time now. Then the music stops. Where's the call centre assistant? Talk to me! An engaged tone. And then the call CUTS OUT. That's when you realize there are no people left anymore. The robots have taken over.

Delivery Fail

A Twitter user shared a picture of a parcel she'd received. When ordering, in the special instructions she'd told the online company she wanted the purchase for a surprise party, and asked if they could make sure it wasn't obvious from the wrapping. They responded by printing her instructions and sticking them on the box.

AI has reached a point where humans are not needed anymore, and the logical next step for them will be to wipe us all out. So forget about rearranging your furniture delivery now. The best thing you can do is keep running, and hope that our robot overlords never find you.

Getting an Elderly Relative on to Facetime

Many people from your uncle's generation have adopted new technology with enthusiasm. They live a happy new life online embracing social media and reviewing local businesses. Sadly, your uncle isn't one of them.

He writes down email addresses in the notebook on his hall table, still sends you cheques for your birthday and signs off text messages with 'Yours sincerely'. But when you explain that he'll cut his landline bills if he installs Facetime, his love of a bargain overcomes his distrust of technology.

He still has the iPad you gave him last Christmas. He keeps it switched off and wrapped in an old cardigan so the Russians can't use it to steal his money. It's not much of a surprise, given that he uses the Kindle you bought him the year before as a bookmark.

Talking him through the process on his landline, you wait as he fetches the iPad and declares that it doesn't work anymore. You explain that it's merely out of charge and wait as he tracks down the charger and plugs it in.

Getting him to tap on the right app and remember his Apple ID is another gruelling test of patience. Eventually, he remembers that he's written the password in his address book right next to his banking one.

You call him and, amazingly, he manages to answer. Yes, you are looking at a close-up of his hairy ear. And yes, he is still talking to you on his landline simultaneously. But it still feels like a breakthrough.

You ask how his week has been, but he doesn't have time to chat, as he'll miss the start of *Countryfile*. You wonder if you should explain streaming, but decide you've both been through quite enough for one day.

YouTube Fail

A Twitter user confessed that he got revenge on his wife after an argument by spending an hour watching Beatles videos on her YouTube account. He explained that she hates the band, and now YouTube will keep suggesting their videos for her.

Putting too much Faith in Your SatNav

You've been using the same TomTom for about ten years now, and you know it's time to replace it. You'd even be better off balancing your phone in the cup holder and using the maps app. But you paid for the SatNav, and you want to get your money's worth before it finally packs in.

Leaving plenty of time before your meeting, you type the postcode in and follow the instructions. You first suspect it might struggle when it leads you past a sign reading 'No through road. Access only'. Trusting your SatNav rather than the sign, you almost crash into a group of angry workers who sarcastically clap as you attempt the 27-point turn out of the narrow space.

Your journey has been pretty smooth since then. You've been zipping down a series of rural roads

that your SatNav has cleverly chosen to help you avoid congested motorways. You wonder which motorways these might be. Maybe you should have checked exactly where you were going first. You force the thought out of your mind. You know your SatNav won't let you down.

It leads you into the middle of a field, and cows gather round to witness your humiliation. You give your SatNav a firm knock, and reverse out. You've been driving for a while since then. You tell yourself that a business park is bound to appear on the horizon at any moment. But the air is getting salty. You can hear gulls overhead. Is that the sound of crashing waves in the distance?

You seem to be joining the queue for a ferry. Surely they would have mentioned if the meeting were in a different country? But it's too late to back down now. You'd rather begin a new life as a farmer in Provence than admit your SatNav got it wrong.

Your phone is buzzing with angry texts now, asking

why you aren't in the meeting, but you ignore them and happily drive onto the boat.

Twitch Fail

A Twitter user confessed that his son had just started to stream himself playing games on Twitch. After two weeks the son was overjoyed to discover he had his first follower. His dad vowed never to admit that it was him.

Trying to Print Something Out

You're about to head to the airport when you remember you need to print your boarding pass.

You cast a sly glance at your printer and your heart sinks.

A few years ago, humanity agreed that creating a machine that could print something out without goading you into a heart attack was never going to happen. Since then, we've found many ingenious ways of cutting out the awful machines. Which makes the few occasions when you still need them all the more unbearable.

You switch your printer on. It runs some slow and noisy checks, relishing the chance to make you wait. You try to send your boarding pass over WiFi, but it's refusing to communicate with your laptop. Bluetooth doesn't work either, so you're forced to root around in your drawer for a lead. You find one, and connect your printer to your laptop. It can't pretend it hasn't got the file now, but that doesn't mean it's ready to play ball just yet. It keeps your document in a queue for five minutes, as though it's got plenty of other important things to do. Finally, the machine clatters into life. It chews up the first attempt, leaving you with a smeared triangle of paper.

You try again, and this time it stops halfway through the QR code, claiming that it's run out of *yellow* ink. You know you've never printed anything yellow, and it knows it too. It just wants you to beg. You get down on your knees, clasp your hands, tell your printer that it's the most important device in your house and you promise you'll never ignore it again.

It grudgingly spits out the rest of your pass. You unplug it, breaking your promise immediately. It's going to remember that when you're in a hurry to print out those concert tickets next month. Oh yes.

Livestreaming Your Life

A few weeks ago, you took the plunge and started vlogging. Sure, you haven't got a lot of views yet. But things will pick up soon, and the millions will pour in from ad revenue. Anyway, you've already invested in some T-shirts and mugs featuring your catchphrase, 'You are awesome-sauce', so you can't back down now.

Facebook Cringe

A Facebook user asked, 'Is that your brother? He looks just like you' on a photo that had just been posted. The reply was, 'That's my girlfriend, dumbass'.

Your pre-recorded vlogs didn't get a lot of views, and the only comments were spam links to cheap Rolexes. So you've changed tactic, and have decided to livestream your life until you get the attention you deserve.

'You guys are so awesome-sauce,' you say as you prepare breakfast, keeping your eyes fixed on the screen and spilling milk all over the counter. And, 'Thank you so much for joining me,' you say as you walk down your street, getting confused glances from onlookers.

'I want you to do something very special for me,' you say in the queue at the coffee shop. 'Please click on the like button and the subscribe button, it means I'll be able to keep bringing you all this great content.' 'Check out the merch link in the description,' you say as you arrive in the office, adding, 'Don't forget you can get 20 per cent off if you use the code OFFER20'. 'But that's a limited time offer,' you explain as you sit at your desk. 'So be quick, people!'

An hour later, one of your colleagues loses it because you won't stop talking into your phone. It makes for a great segment, and might even work in your channel trailer.

Soon after you've arrived home, your parents call and say they've been watching you on their computer and they're worried. Perhaps it would be a good idea to turn your phone off and have a nice lie down? You consider this for a moment. Maybe they're right. Not everyone has to be an online celebrity. And you could be putting too much pressure on yourself by trying too hard.

There's only one way to find out. 'What do you guys think?' you bark at your screen. 'Leave a comment and I'll read the best ones out later.' There's no way back now. You'll still be shouting 'Remember to like and subscribe' as you're dragged away and sedated.

Emoji Fail

A Twitter user revealed that her mother had taken to ending her texts with rows of the poo emoji. She thought they were chocolate kisses.

Forgetting Your Password

You're about to buy some new trousers when the website asks for your password. You haven't used the site for a few months, but you're sure you'll be able to remember which one you used.

You're drawing a blank. You take your cyber security seriously, so you don't use the same passwords for everything, or something idiotic like 'password' or '123456'. So what did you use? You try the name of your first dog. Rocky was always such a loyal friend. Perhaps he'll come to your rescue once more. Nope.

How could you have forgotten such an important thing so quickly? Maybe you accidentally saved over it in your brain when you memorized all those capital cities for the Zoom quiz.

You know you once created a password based around your favourite colour, but you can't remember which website it was for, or what that colour was. You try a couple of combinations based around blue and purple, but zilch.

Why would it matter if hackers got into your account anyway? It's not as if you saved your card details. The worst they could do is put in their own card details and buy you something you don't want.

You try a couple of attempts based around your mother's maiden name, but they don't work either. You're locked out, and now you'll have to go through the humiliation of resetting a password you were sure you'd remember. You follow the link to the reset page. This time you come up with something based on the name of a childhood friend and your old street number, something which no one could ever guess, but you could never forget.

You type it in. The site says it can't accept this password because it's identical to your current one.

Instagram Fail

An Instagram user posted a picture of herself wearing sunglasses in a convertible car. Eagle-eyed viewers zoomed into the reflection in her lenses to show that her boyfriend was rather dangerously taking her photo while driving.

Arranging a Parcel Delivery

You've found a book about starting a veg patch that will be the perfect gift for your mum, so you fill out your address and card details. The last part of the form asks what they should do with the parcel if you're out.

Maybe they could just leave it on your doorstep. It's not like any of the local thieves are going to be interested in carrots. But then again, they won't know what's inside the parcel until they've stolen and opened it, which means you'll end up having to root around the local fly-tipping hot spots when they throw it away.

OK. Maybe they could leave it at the side of the house. But you've tried that before. The delivery was followed by hours of torrential rain that reduced the parcel and its contents to mush. Or what about hiding it in the recycling bin? No, you know how that will end. With you racing down the street and yelling frantically at the bin men because you forgot about it.

So just make sure you're in when it arrives. And yes, you are in … on the toilet. You race downstairs, frantically yelling at them to leave the parcel, but when you get to the door all you find is a card telling you to collect it from their depot, which is 40 miles away and open between 8a.m. and 8:04a.m. on the last Thursday of every month.

Looks like you're going to have to email a gift voucher again.

Email Fail

A Twitter user described how she had intended to type 'I am afraid I'll have to postpone our meeting', but pressed send too soon so that the message simply read, 'I am afraid'. A quick follow-up was needed to clarify that this wasn't actually a cry for help.

Relying on Google Too Much

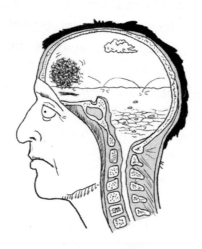

Since Google came along, you've become so clever that the professor of braininess at Smartypants University would want to copy your homework. You can settle any argument in a second. You can even butt in on the conversations of others with your fact-checking skills, which of course they love.

You don't wear glasses, but if you did you'd be constantly shoving them up the bridge of your nose and grinning smugly. But you're worried you've come to rely on Google so much that you don't actually know *anything* anymore. You decide to go cold turkey and prove your brain can still work without it.

- A stranger stops and asks you for directions. Without Google Maps, you have no idea where anything is, so you point them in a random direction. The same stranger angrily beeps as they pass you again ten minutes later.

- An argument about the score of a previous Champions League final breaks out among your friends. They look to you for an answer, but you can only offer a vague guess, and the row spills over into violence.

- Your son asks what clouds are, and you have to admit that, despite having looked at the things for almost three decades, you have genuinely no idea. You get to witness the exact moment when a child realizes a parent isn't an all-knowing god, but just another clueless idiot.

It turns out your brain doesn't work at all without Google. Years of reliance on the Internet has turned it to useless mush, with less memory than a ZX81. Your experiment has ended in failure. It's time to get back online before everyone realizes that you've become little more than a phone holder with a built-in speaker.

Being Recorded for Training Purposes

Waiting to be put through to a customer support line, you're warned that your call might be recorded for training purposes.

You vow to be a model caller, imagining a packed lecture hall at Customer Support University, where they play your call and the professor says, 'and THAT is how you do it', and the entranced students rise and applaud.

The assistant asks for your name. You have a fairly common one, and you speak clearly, but they have no idea what you're saying. You try to spell it out, but go blank on the phonetic alphabet. The students at Call Centre University are not going to be impressed.

With your name finally established, you describe your problem. They read through a script that begins with them saying how sorry they are about it, but they clearly have no more idea than you do how to solve it. So you're put back on hold for a few minutes, then transferred to another department. The new department can't help either, and have no idea why you were referred.

Zoom Win

A Twitter business-user described how they've trained their children to interrupt Zoom meetings when they simply can't take any more waffle. The children are summoned by WhatsApp message, and get an extra £1 pocket money for each disruption.

You're switched back to the original department, but to a new assistant who also reacts in confusion to your incredibly simple name. You're clutching your phone so tightly your knuckles are going white. But you must keep it together. You don't want this recording to become the stock example of a psycho customer losing it.

You're put on hold *again*, and speak to yet another assistant. Your temples are throbbing and your lips are ripped back tight over your teeth as you go through the whole name thing again. You try to hold it in, you really do, but when assistant number 48 goes through the same script about being sorry, you say they're not sorry, you just want them to … PLEASE … SOLVE … THE… SODDING… PROBLEM. And *they* hang up on you.

Now you realize what really goes on in staff training. They teach them how to push customers until they have such a violent meltdown that it's OK for them to end the call. With total justification.

Multiscreening

You're settling down to watch the season finale of a popular drama series. You've heard so many theories about how it's going to end, and you can't wait to find out which is right. But there's something missing, and it takes you a while to realize what it is. You're only looking at one screen. Sure, it's nice to give your full attention to something in theory, but it feels very odd when you actually do it.

You get your phone out and Tweet your reaction to the show as it happens. A friend texts to let you know they're watching it with a few others on Zoom, so you drag your laptop over and click on the invite link. This is great. What could have been a quiet night in has been transformed into a social occasion.

An actor appears on screen, and you know you recognize them from somewhere, but you can't quite remember where. You fetch your iPad and prop it next to you with a cushion so you can keep IMDB open.

You're now interested to know how the show is going down with your Facebook friends, but you don't want to miss anything on Twitter, so you get your old phone out of the kitchen drawer and balance it on your lap.

Every time you add a screen, your experience is getting more exciting. There's no point stopping now. You turn on your Switch so you can have a quick game of Zelda too. Then you drag your old TV and DVD player down from the attic and make your way through your *Friends* box set at the same time. Connecting a monitor to your laptop helps to fill a gap on your left, and an old eReader will have to do for the one on your right.

It's still not enough. There are spaces around you with no screens. You go online and order twelve new TVs. As soon as they arrive, you'll finally be able to relax.

Facebook Fail

In 2014, a Facebook user only found out that his parents had divorced when his mum changed her relationship status to 'single'.

Reading Product Reviews

Your current toaster is slightly too small for the type of bread you buy, so there's a cold strip at the top of every slice. You find a new toaster that seems bigger, but you're not quite sure it will solve the problem. Perhaps the reviews will help.

The first gives it five stars, because it has a 'dial on the side you can adjust depending on how you want your toast done'. Don't all toasters have this? Has this reviewer just switched from holding slices of bread over an open fire on a fork?

The next gives it one star, because its colour doesn't quite match their kettle. You have neither their kettle nor apparent OCD, so you ignore this.

The next is also negative, because 'the packaging was damaged when I received it'. Who cares about toaster packaging? Do people keep them untouched in their boxes in the hope they'll be worth money one day like *Star Wars* figures?

Zoom Fail

A Reddit user shared a screen
shot of an embarrassing moment
in her Zoom class. She wrote 'I
hate this class' in the chat bar,
thinking she was in iMessage.
She then pretended she'd meant
to write 'I love this class'.

Then a positive one. The reviewer says the toaster arrived on time, and has given them no problems in the month they've been using it. They seem trustworthy, so you click through to their other reviews. They have also given five stars to an 8-foot gummy snake, a pair of giant lobster claws that fit over your hands and a cat brush that fits over your tongue so your pet thinks you're licking them. Ho hum.

You read a hundred reviews, and not one of them mentions that it won't toast a large slice of bread. You go ahead and you buy it. It arrives with the packaging intact, in a colour that doesn't offend you and it does, indeed, have a dial on the side. But it still won't heat your bread properly. You will hate those 100 idiotic, useless strangers every time you bite into that cold, disappointing end of your toast.

Avoiding Email Scams

An urgent message comes through from your bank. Someone has just tried to withdraw a large sum of money, and you know it wasn't you, so you click the link to enter your details and …

Wait a minute. This isn't really from your bank. You're pretty sure they'd be able to spell 'verification', and there's no way their email address is 'FatGareth1991@yahoo.com'. You delete the email. Who'd fall for that scam?

The next day you get a personal message from Beyoncé on Twitter. She needs to borrow some money for her airfare, but she'll pay you back and even perform a special show in your city. How nice of her to contact fans directly like this ...

Hang on. If that's really Beyoncé, why does she only have twelve followers? Another close one. Soon after, you're contacted about a long-lost relative who has died and left you a mega huge inheritance. Obviously, they'll need a transaction fee to get the money into your account, but what's a few thousand compared with the riches you're about to inherit? This time you're halfway through filling in your details before you realize ...

You resolve to be much more vigilant from now on. Your electricity provider emails you with a bill, but you have no way of knowing if it's really them. You ignore it, plus all the reminders that follow. And now you're about to confirm your online grocery order when ... you realize you could be about to give your hard-earned money to a Russian teenager who creates convincing spoof sites. Then you try to check your bank balance, but can't shake the notion that it isn't quite safe. Someone, somewhere is watching you, and they are going to take your money.

Six months later, you're living in a cold house, eating beans from a can by candlelight and grasping a baseball bat to protect the wads of banknotes under your bed. You haven't slept for days, and you have scurvy. But at least you're safe from cybercriminals.

Hearing a Default Ringtone

● ● ● ● ● ● ● ● ● ● ● ● ● ● ● ● ● ●

In a queue at the supermarket, you hear a noise that sets you on edge. It's a default mobile ringtone, the sound of a serene robot playing the marimba just before killing you. Everyone else fishes around in their pockets and handbags, and you watch them with pity.

Text Fail

A Tumblr user texted his friend to say that his first date had gone well, and he had kissed the girl in the woods on the way home. Unfortunately, autocorrect changed 'kissed' to 'killed'.

These people actually keep the default settings on their phones. As well as having the same ringtone as everyone else, causing them unnecessary strife at moments like this, they probably keep the same pinging text notification and the same wallpaper of moving blobs. They've probably even kept their keyboard clicks on, the poor, ridiculous yokels.

You imagine the swoosh of their sent emails, the harsh radar beeps of their morning alarms and the jarring tri-tone of their voicemail notifications. And look at those phone covers. Clear plastic cases that look as though they've been scratched by velociraptors and faux-leather wallets they have frayed to reveal the cardboard inside. One even has no cover at all, meaning the phone will be perfectly safe as long as it isn't dropped from a height of more than 3 millimetres.

They've all checked their phones and the horrible marimba is still playing. The woman behind you nudges you and scowls. You whip your phone out of your pocket and stare at it in horror. You forgot – last night you accidentally returned the settings to default.

Zoom Fail

The foreign affairs editor of Sky News went viral in 2020 when her son interrupted her live on TV to ask if he could have two biscuits. It wasn't clear if it was a genuine accident, or if he'd cunningly picked the moment he was most likely to get a 'Yes, now please piss off'.

Discovering a New Gadget

As an ex-user of Google Glass, Nokia N-Gage and the Facebook Phone, you've backed the wrong technology in the past. But you can't be wrong this time. You've just seen a 3D printer you can afford, and you can't let yourself get left behind.

You drive off to buy it, wondering if it's the last thing you'll ever need. You'll now be able to make your own bowls, cutlery, combs, tools, door handles and anything else you can think of. They even use these things in medicine, don't they? Maybe you won't even need a doctor anymore. If you break your leg or your heart conks out, you'll be able to print yourself a new one and carry on. And if a robber breaks in, you can simply print a samurai sword and chase them away.

Email Fail

A US student tried to motivate herself to get her final assignment of the year finished by calling it 'LAST PAPER BITCHES!!!' Unfortunately, she forgot to change the title before submitting it.

This is just the start. Soon, you'll be printing out clothes, furniture and even food. Every day will be 3D Christmas, as your new best friend spews out an endless stream of luxury items.

You arrive home, download the software, assemble the printer and load the filament. You watch in fascination as it builds an actual solid cube, layer by layer. A week later, you're surrounded by white lumps of plastic that you don't quite know what to do with. You've made an Eiffel Tower, pencil holder, the entire Fellowship of the Ring and you're running out of desk space. You start to wonder if this is another one of those inventions you don't really, actually need.

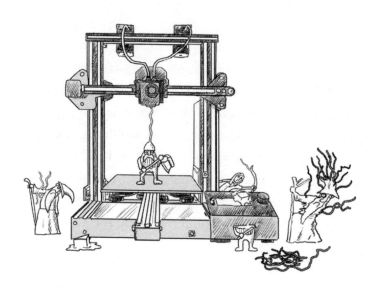

A burglar strikes the following night, and rudely refuses to wait for you to make a samurai sword. They take everything except the 3D printer.

Realizing You Live in the Future

Your train is about to pull into the station. You've never been to the city, and have a bit of spare time before your meeting, so you ask your Facebook followers for recommendations of places to eat. You jokingly address them as 'hive mind', but as the replies come in, you have a strange moment of epiphany. They really are a hive mind. You're living in a science fiction world where everyone can transmit their thoughts instantly in a weird sort of telepathy.

You're hurtling across the ground, staring at a glowing screen that can tell you anything, and put you in touch with anyone. This is the future. You've spent the last three decades so annoyed that proper hoverboards never became real that you never stopped to appreciate what *did* happen.

Zoom Fail

In 2021, an Ohio State Senator used a virtual background of his home office to try to cover up the fact he was driving during a Zoom call. However, his seat belt could clearly be seen, and he kept leaning forward to look from left to right.

You update your status, announcing to everyone that you've just realized how amazing technology is, and how lucky we all are be alive in this age of wonders. One friend comments to say they hate Big Tech. Another complains about the coverage of their network. Another friend says their DMs are open if you're having a funny turn and need someone to contact. Your uncle calls you a 'snowflake' and your vegan colleague steps in to defend you. They're soon arguing about Winston Churchill, somehow.

A spam account you added by mistake is now urging you to invest in Bitcoin.

You sigh. It doesn't look like anyone is going

to share your moment. But perhaps it's not in the nature of humans to be content. If this ungrateful lot had been given hoverboards, they'd only be complaining about the battery life.

You decide to keep it to yourself from now on. But you haven't changed your mind. Technology is really rather brilliant, despite everything.

Zoom Fail

A Twitter user was surprised to see their colleagues smiling every time they took a sip of tea in a Zoom meeting. It turned out their partner had given them a mug with 'I'm a Twat' written on the bottom.